POSTCARD HISTORY SERIES

Gloucester and Cape Ann

CAPE ANN, MASSACHUSETTS. First named Cape Ann in the 1600s by James I of England, this peninsula was previously home to indigenous peoples before European colonists first visited the region between 1605 and 1606. Additionally, the region is home to Gloucester, which in 1623 became the first permanent settlement in the Massachusetts Bay Colony. (Courtesy of the author.)

ON THE COVER: Though one may credit schooners and other technology or vessels used for harvesting large catches of fish, the Cape Ann fisherman bears the most credit for making Gloucester home to the tile of "America's Oldest Seaport," as these fishermen's grit and determination are ultimately responsible for allowing Gloucester to maintain a strong maritime economy and culture. (Both, courtesy of the author.)

POSTCARD HISTORY SERIES

Gloucester and Cape Ann

Ryan A. McRae

ARCADIA
PUBLISHING

Published by Arcadia Publishing
Charleston, South Carolina

Printed in the United States of America

Library of Congress Control Number: 2024930306

For all general information contact Arcadia Publishing at:
Telephone 843-853-2070
Fax 843-853-0044
E-mail sales@arcadiapublishing.com

Visit us on the Internet at www.arcadiapublishing.com

I dedicate this book to all of my relatives, ancestors, and the future generations of my family in honor of our centuries-long roots in Gloucester.

CONTENTS

ACKNOWLEDGMENTS

I would like to thank all of my family members, especially my doting and loving parents, David McRae and Angela (Heaton) McRae, and my devoted and cherished grandmother Sharon (Ilges) McRae. Over the course of my life, they have all provided me with excellent stories that helped me find the inspiration for this book and enthusiasm for Cape Ann's history. I love you three beyond measure and will always be grateful for our close relationships. I will always keep that in my heart. Hearing family stories about the generations who built Gloucester and who are long gone (such as the past members of the McRae, Ilges, Conant, Veno, Wonson, Morrow, Proctor, and Doucette families) helped me find the desire to make sure Gloucester's own story is told and that our family (and my patriline) will have a permanent stamp on the city's history. I also want to thank my dear aunts, uncles, great-aunts, great-uncles, cousins, extended family members, and friends for contributing to my love of these stories and always sharing insight I find so special. I love you all and look forward to one day sharing this with the future generations of our family.

In addition, I would like to thank all of the staff I worked with at Arcadia Publishing to make this book a possibility. I would also like to thank many members of the historical community of Gloucester (and other towns on or near Cape Ann) who were able to tell me more about this region and its past or happily encourage me and support my endeavors. Being someone who has 400 years of ancestry in Gloucester (especially as a direct descendant of Roger Conant), having the ability to tell the story of this community, and feel welcome doing it, is very special. I will always be proud of this project and hope the community will be as well. I thank you all for your support.

All postcard images in this book appear courtesy of the author.

Introduction

An island peninsula nestled in Northeastern Massachusetts, Cape Ann, formerly known as Avalonia and Wagawam by the land's indigenous forebears, was first inhabited by Native Americans by approximately 3,000 BC. The peninsula was especially home to members of the Pawtucket tribe, who established settlements along the Essex and Annisquam Rivers, along with members of the Massachusett, Nipmuc, Penacook, and Wampanoag tribes, who also resided in nearby areas. Additionally, the indigenous community that existed here prior to European colonization was known for spending summers on the peninsula and bringing elements of Abenaki Native American culture to this region. In support of this evidence, on Cape Ann, toward the western side of the peninsula, one can find pottery, arrowheads, and other objects that represent the indigenous society and culture that existed prior to European colonization. With that being said, the first encounter between the indigenous population and Europeans occurred between 1605 and 1606, when Samuel de Champlain, a European explorer, first mapped the area. Champlain had peaceful relationships with these Natives, and he personally noted the area's wide, scenic coastline and open harbor (the location of Gloucester Harbor), which he referred to as "le beau port." Eventually, within a decade of Champlain's initial encounter, the peninsula was claimed by English colonists and was proclaimed Cape Tragabigzanda in 1613 by an English captain, John Smith, in honor of a Turkish companion of his. The peninsula was soon renamed Cape Ann by King James I of England, who named this area after his wife, Anne of Denmark.

Though the Pawtucket people had initially coexisted with Europeans, once the English colonists had settled on the peninsula and in the general vicinity in the 1610s, wars broke out between Natives and Europeans that led many indigenous people to flee to northern areas. Unfortunately, this, along with severe disease outbreaks, caused a massive population decline within the indigenous community of Cape Ann. With the indigenous population mostly deceased from these wars and outbreaks, by 1623, Cape Ann was sparsely populated and became a sought-after land to settle on due to the bountiful fish catches that were said to be had off the peninsula's coast. This led to a group of English settlers led by Roger Conant, all of whom were escaping stringent laws in England that suppressed their freedoms, to land at present-day Gloucester and establish a settlement. The colonists began their settlement in approximately April 1623, naming it Gloucester by December 1623. Gloucester then became the Massachusetts Bay Colony's first permanent formal settlement (a fact also noted on Stage Fort Park Tablet in Gloucester). This first attempt at settling Gloucester failed, but colonists once again formed a settlement in the location two decades later that was permanently incorporated as the town of Gloucester in 1642. After Gloucester's incorporation, it was led by Puritan colonists in an "open-town" type of government for the first 200 years of its existence, as was common in the Massachusetts Bay Colony at that time. Additionally, the communities of Manchester-by-the-Sea (initially known as Jeoffereye's Creek), and Essex (first known as Chebacco) formed on the outskirts of the peninsula. Several other hamlets and villages came into existence in the 1700s, such as Sandy Bay, which eventually became an independent town in 1840 and would later be renamed Rockport.

However, regardless of the other growth that occurred on the peninsula, at this time, the fishing industry in this region became paramount to all industrial and economic activity, helping Gloucester earn its distinction as "America's Oldest Seaport." Additionally, with the continued population growth and the development of the schooner fishing tradition, by the late 1800s, Gloucester and Cape Ann began drawing immigrants as well as entrepreneurs seeking opportunities in the maritime industry. The population growth led to the formation of several distinct communities within Gloucester as well as Cape Ann, including East Gloucester, West Gloucester, Annisquam, Lanesville, Dogtown, Riverdale, and Magnolia, all of which came into existence by at least 1850. Furthermore, Gloucester faced its largest growth in population between 1870 and 1900 and developed immensely at that time, especially drawing in immigrants of French Canadian, Portuguese, and Italian origin. With its population spike, Gloucester was incorporated formally as a city in 1873 and continued to develop its harbor, infrastructure, and general cityscape while different European cultures blended within the city's boundaries.

In addition to the noted maritime enterprises that made up the region's economy, Gloucester and Cape Ann both gained notoriety in the late 1800s and early 1900s for becoming widely sought-after summer destinations for wealthy residents of large cities in the Northeastern United States. This industry led to the area hosting numerous elegant and grandiose summer resorts that drew countless artists, authors, scholars, and other socialites to Gloucester and Cape Ann. This industry therefore marked a shift in Cape Ann's path, as the region became just as reliant on tourism as it did on fishing. It also drew in new people who established art colonies, galleries, and other businesses on the peninsula. Additionally, with the tourism economy on Cape Ann holding the presence it did, this allowed other small towns and communities on the peninsula, such as Rockport and Manchester-by-the-Sea, to become their own distinct communities aside from Gloucester. For example, Rockport became an eclectic town known for its artisan businesses and quaint, picturesque natural sites (similar to Essex), while Manchester-by-the-Sea became home to numerous cottages that made the town its own summer destination for socialites. Eventually though, toward the mid-20th century, summer tourism declined in the area, leading to the removal, redevelopment, or destruction of numerous luxurious seaside resorts that once lined Cape Ann's shores. However, even with the maritime and hospitality industries not holding the precedence they once did in the area, Cape Ann still maintains notoriety for its unique roots and history in these sectors and continues to boast a fine arts, architectural, historical, and cultural landscape that is noted throughout New England and the Northeastern United States in the present day.

One

SCHOONERS
AND LIGHTHOUSES
MARITIME SCENES OF CAPE ANN

With Gloucester and Cape Ann's notoriety as a maritime destination comes a wide variety of scenes, places, and people that represent its distinct roots in that industry. Fishermen, for example, were the backbone of Cape Ann's fishing industry that brought economic stability to the region for centuries, and their sacrifices and dedicated labor have been recognized through the numerous monuments, artworks, literary pieces, and folk figures inspired by them. For example, one folk figure, "Old Salt," a Gloucester fisherman whose exact identity is unknown for sure, was featured on numerous postcards, advertisements, and artworks and represented the grit, sacrifices, and personalities of the fishermen in this industry. Additionally, beyond the representation of fishermen came the recognition of their sacrifices; fishing, albeit still a difficult and tedious task, was once a more deadly industry since boats and schooners did not have modern technology to protect ships or crews. At the same time, even with its dangers came the reality that many of these fishermen had to feed their families, leading to their participation in this industry. As a result, an estimated 10,000 Gloucester fishermen have perished in shipwrecks. However, their sacrifices do not go unnoticed; in 1923, Gloucester erected the Gloucester Fishermen's Memorial, also known as "the Man at the Wheel," in honor of Gloucester fishermen who have been lost at sea.

Though many of Gloucester's maritime-themed places of heritage revolve around fishermen, there are a plethora of other sites, such as the six lighthouses that line Cape Ann's shores, that also represent the other aspects of the area's fishing industry. These lighthouses and early lifesaving stations (which existed mostly prior to the official creation of the US Coast Guard in 1915) were essential to protecting sailors and crews, ensuring their safe passage, and helping prevent the deaths of many fishermen at sea. In addition to these lighthouses that now draw tourists for their nautical charm, Gloucester Harbor also hosts scenes of the region's maritime roots, being home to numerous docks, piers, and an active port that, in the past, has seen many schooners bring profitable catches back to be sold worldwide; it continues to be home to fishing businesses and attractions as well.

THE MAN AND HIS NETS, GLOUCESTER, 1905 (LEFT), AND OLD FISHERMAN, GLOUCESTER, 1907. As Gloucester is known as "America's Oldest Seaport," the city is home to one of the most historic fishing industries in the United States. With that being said, with the designation as one of the nation's busiest and most popular seaports comes a strong maritime economy, which built the Cape Ann region from the 1600s to the 20th century. Furthermore, this industry created a network of thousands of fishermen of various ethnicities who diligently served on schooners and commercial boats. They sacrificed their own time, and in the case of approximately 10,000 fishermen, their own lives, to bring catches back to Gloucester to be sold worldwide and to bring economic prosperity to the community.

GLOUCESTER FISHING SCHOONER, GLOUCESTER, MASS.

A GLOUCESTER SCHOONER, 1915.
The schooner, a wooden fishing craft, was the most popular vessel used by Gloucester's sailors for fishing due to its nautical speed and was Gloucester's economic lifeline when the city relied on its maritime industry for economic prosperity. As schooners are seen as significant in building Gloucester's status as a famed seaport, enthusiasts celebrate schooners and their history during the Gloucester Schooner Festival, which is held annually every September.

THEY THAT GO
DOWN TO THE SEA
IN SHIPS
1623 — 1923

GLOUCESTER FISHERMEN'S MEMORIAL, 1960. The Gloucester Fishermen's Memorial, known as the "Man at the Wheel," was designed by Leonard F. Craske and was erected in 1923. Located along Stacy Boulevard in Gloucester, this monument lists the names of Gloucester fishermen who have died at sea during the city's nearly 400-year history and is also known for becoming an icon for Gloucester's maritime history.

Harbor and Wharf Scene, Gloucester, Mass.

11-22-06 ESM

GLOUCESTER HARBOR'S WHARVES, 1906 (ABOVE), AND GLOUCESTER'S FISHING PIERS, 1948. As Gloucester Harbor was first noted in maps by the French explorer Samuel de Champlain between 1605 and 1606, early European settlers who visited Gloucester quickly realized its prime location for a fishing settlement due to its wide open bay. After English settlers created their settlement in 1623, Gloucester Harbor became the center of a new village that became known for its fishing industry, which especially became more successful once the town was officially incorporated in 1642 and was permanently occupied. Currently, the harbor is known for its divided Inner and Outer Harbors, which are made up of several different coves and wharves, but is also home to numerous commercial and private docks as well.

The Fish Pier, Gloucester, Mass.

UNLOADING GORTON'S FISH, 1906. After voyages into the Atlantic Ocean, which often took schooners and fishing boats miles into the sea, fishermen landed their catches at Gloucester Harbor to begin the process of cleaning, drying, and packaging these fish for market or sale to far-away destinations. Most often, these catches included fish such as cod and halibut, as they were plentiful off the Cape Ann coast and were easy to dry and preserve.

CLEANING FISH, GLOUCESTER, 1907. After bringing loads of fish back to port, fishermen had the task of cleaning and gutting fish to prepare them for sale. Cleaning fish was the first task in processing catches and involved removing skin, cutting meat, and preparing meat to be dried. These tasks often occurred alongside the fishing port, in various warehouses, or along fishing docks in "fish yards."

9753. DRYING FISH. GLOUCESTER. MASS.

DRYING FISH, GLOUCESTER, 1906. After fishermen brought their catches back to port, following cleaning the fish, fishermen often dried their catches on racks to cure fish meat and prepare these meats for being salted and packed for shipment. Drying fish was popular, as it allowed meat to be preserved for longer periods of time, but it had to be done carefully, and tediously, to ensure the meat would not spoil.

Flake Yard No. 1, Gorton-Pew Co. Gloucester, Mass. 214124

GORTON'S FLAKE YARD NO. 1, GLOUCESTER, 1907. The final step in this process, once strips of fish meat were done drying on racks and had cured, they were then known as "fish flakes." These flakes were often salted and packed and were known for their ability to stay preserved for long periods of time, making them popular for sailors at sea, as well as less wealthy individuals who bought them because of their affordability.

FISH WAREHOUSES. GLOUCESTER. MASS.

FISH WAREHOUSES, 1920. Along the ocean in Gloucester, one can notice the many piers and docks that line the coast, and they are bordered by many warehouses where fishermen process their catches and prepare fish for the market. Though some seafood businesses in Gloucester today use warehouses to ice or measure fish, many of Gloucester's major fish-producing companies of past eras would bring cleaned or dried fish into these buildings to be packed and shipped to destinations worldwide, and they would often have salt boxes in these buildings to hold their newly landed fish as well to preserve them. These warehouses have become less prevalent in Gloucester, since many have been demolished or were destroyed in previous eras. However, these buildings still remain an important part of Gloucester's fishing industry, since they housed operations for many of the city's vital seafood companies.

CLAM DIGGERS, 1905. Though Gloucester and Cape Ann's maritime economy largely centered around the catching of fish and lobster, clams and other shellfish were harvested manually by diggers. This aspect of Cape Ann's maritime economy was largely overshadowed by the more lucrative off-coast fishing operations, but clam diggers often covered Cape Ann's many beaches in search of shellfish that were then sold at market or through various seafood shops in the area.

LOBSTERMAN'S SHANTIES   2562

LOBSTERMEN'S SHANTIES, CAPE ANN, 1950. Just as fishermen housed their buckets and cleaning tools in sheds or warehouses near docks and ports, lobstermen held traps and other materials in sheds and "shanties" near their workplaces as well. These shanties were often poorly built, temporary structures that could be found on the beaches and docks of Cape Ann, where lobstermen processed their catches and sent them to market.

CAPE ANN LOBSTER GREETING, 1973 (ABOVE), AND MELLOW'S LOBSTERS OF GLOUCESTER, 1948. Though Cape Ann is long known for its lobster production, lobster meat was not considered a delicacy until the 1880s. Prior to that point, lobster was served to prisoners, servants, and paupers regularly due to the abundance of them in New England waters. However, in the 1600s, 1700s, and early 1800s, lobster was still eaten plentifully by area residents, especially poorer fishermen, who easily found the creatures along the area's shores. Eventually, toward the early 20th century, the demand for lobster vastly increased in North America when the meat became popular among socialites. Lobsters then skyrocketed in value, and with their population still high off the Massachusetts coast, this led locals to take advantage of the lucrative lobster market and establish businesses in the area, such as Mellow's Lobsters, which operated in Gloucester in the mid-1900s.

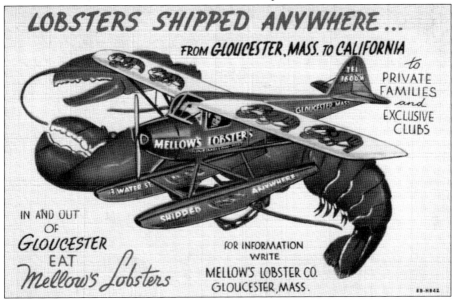

ITALIAN FISHING BOATS, GLOUCESTER, MASS.

ITALIAN FISHING BOATS, GLOUCESTER, 1920. In the late 19th and early 20th centuries, Gloucester saw an influx of Portuguese and Italian immigrants into the city and the general vicinity of Cape Ann. The immigration levels into Gloucester were a controversial topic at the time and drew the ire of many citizens, who enacted discriminatory practices against immigrants of Italian or Portuguese ethnicity, many of which practices were especially seen in the hiring process for jobs. With that being said, with limited employment options, many of the newcomers went to work in manual labor fields, and numerous immigrants began to work in the local maritime industry. Eventually, as the immigrant community in the region continued to increase in the late 1800s, by the early 20th century, Gloucester's maritime industry was made up of many European immigrants who flocked to the area for the promise of work, many of whom began their own fishing operations on Cape Ann as well.

STEAMBOAT WHARF, GLOUCESTER, 1907. Along with the railways, Gloucester residents were able to travel beyond Cape Ann by steamboat. As was common in most of the nation at the time, the steamboat was a popular choice for travelers in the late 1800s and early 1900s due to its affordability and convenience. From Gloucester, steamboat trips ran every day to Boston and Fall River. Here, crowds are seen at Gloucester's steamboat wharf awaiting transportation to Boston.

THE STEAMBOAT *CAPE ANN*, 1910. The SS *Cape Ann* was one of two steamboats that operated out of Gloucester and that was named for the general area, along with the SS *City of Gloucester*. The SS *Cape Ann* was in service between 1895 and 1917 and served the North Shore region, offering daily fares from Gloucester to Boston for 50¢ during the summer months.

MISSING.

A schooner-rigged Boat, 18 ft. long, black outside, left Gloucester for Boston at 12 M., Sunday, June 25, and has not since been heard from.

The only person aboard was a man—dark complexion, about 19 yrs. old and 5 ft. 7 tall.

Any information in regard to the boat or the occupant will be thankfully received by

JOS. A. MOORE, City Marshal.

Gloucester, June 30, 1876.

MISSING SCHOONER POSTAL CARD, 1876. The American "postal card" (as it was first known) became a popular communication medium around 1875. Interestingly, shortly after their inception, townsfolk began to use them as a way to bring awareness to town events and exchange news. This same concept was used by fishermen who sent the cards in the event a boat or crew went missing, which can be seen in this 1876 notice of a missing schooner from Gloucester Harbor.

LIFE SAVING STATION, GLOUCESTER, MASS.

LIFESAVING STATION, GLOUCESTER, 1920. Similar to the lighthouse stations located across Cape Ann to assist sailors with navigation and steer them away from dangers, lifesaving stations were essential to rescuing crews stranded off the area's shores. These stations were built by the US Life-Saving Service, founded in 1878, and many stations were located along the shores of the United States before this service became part of the US Coast Guard in 1915.

The Start of the Life-bout, Life-saving Crew, Dollivar's Neck, Gloucester, Mass.

LIFESAVING CREW (ABOVE) AND RETURN OF THE CREW, GLOUCESTER, 1906. Dolliver's Neck is a small patch of land that forms Gloucester's Freshwater Cove and stretches into the Atlantic Ocean off the western side of Gloucester Harbor. With its prime location on the edge of Gloucester Harbor, Dolliver's Neck served as the inspiration for the US Life-Saving Service to construct a station there in 1900, which opened in 1901. It was officially known as the Gloucester Station Site, and this lifesaving station housed crews who performed rescues off eastern Cape Ann's shores. The station was eventually demolished in approximately 1974, with its buildings being intentionally burned. A new lifesaving station was constructed in a different location in Gloucester soon afterward; it is still active today and is operated by the US Coast Guard.

The Return from the Wreck, Life-saving Crew, Dollivar's Neck, Gloucester, Mass.

OUTWARD BOUND

TEN POUND ISLAND LIGHT, GLOUCESTER, MASS.

123442

TEN POUND ISLAND LIGHT, 1920 (ABOVE), AND TEN POUND ISLAND LIGHTHOUSE, 1905. First built in 1821, the Ten Pound Island Lighthouse was initially a stone structure with an adjacent granite oil house and a lighthouse keeper's residence. After 60 years, the original lighthouse was demolished, and a cast iron tower was put in its place in 1881 on the original foundation; this tower still stands today. In 1889, a fishery was added, and in 1925, during the US Prohibition years, an air station was added to the station to monitor traffic in Gloucester Harbor. The light station itself was decommissioned in 1956, when a light was instead installed on a bell tower on the island. Eventually, the site fell into disrepair, which led the Lighthouse Preservation Society to initiate a project to restore the lighthouse, which was completed in 1989. Several other buildings on the station have been renovated as well.

Ten-pound Island Light, Gloucester, Mass.

65120

Annisquam Light, Gloucester, Mass.

670 1.

ANNISQUAM LIGHTHOUSE, 1905 (ABOVE), AND ANNISQUAM LIGHT, 1945. Located on Wigwam Point in the Annisquam section of Gloucester, this lighthouse was originally built in 1801 and is one of the oldest lighthouses in the state of Massachusetts. Similar to the other lighthouses on Cape Ann, this lighthouse tower has been rebuilt numerous times; the first tower, a wooden structure, was replaced in 1851 by another wooden lighthouse, which was also eventually destroyed in 1897. The present brick lighthouse, built in 1898, was constructed on the original 1801 foundation and still stands today. It was automated in 1974 and was the first lighthouse on Cape Ann to receive automatic lighting. It has been occupied by the US Coast Guard since 1974, and its interior is closed to the public.

ANNISQUAM LIGHT, GLOUCESTER, MASS., CAPE ANN.   919-A

GLOUCESTER, MASS.   Eastern Point Light—Gloucester Harbor.

EASTERN POINT LIGHTHOUSE AND BREAKWATER, 1905 (ABOVE), AND EASTERN POINT LIGHTHOUSE AND BREAKWATER, 1935. Established in 1832, the Eastern Point Lighthouse was constructed when water traffic increased on Cape Ann in the early 19th century. The original tower was poorly built, and the need for a new tower became apparent when the region continued to grow by the mid-19th century and more traffic was coming in and out of Gloucester Harbor. The tower of the lighthouse was reconstructed in 1848, but this version was demolished less than five decades later. In 1890, the third and present lighthouse tower was built on the original foundation. It was automated in 1986 and is currently owned by the US Coast Guard, with its interior closed to the public. Additionally, both the locally famous Dog Reef Breakwater and Mother Ann rock formations are located adjacent to the lighthouse station.

EASTERN POINT LIGHT. GLOUCESTER. MASS   5

THE BREAKWATER AT SUNSET, EASTERN POINT, GLOUCESTER, MASS.

THE DOG BAR BREAKWATER, 1920 (ABOVE), AND THE DOG BAR BREAKWATER, 1950. The Dog Bar Breakwater, constructed between 1894 and 1905, was built by the US Army Corps of Engineers using locally sourced rocks from the Rockport Granite Company. The breakwater's construction stemmed from the struggles of Gloucester residents, who sought the creation of a barge to protect Gloucester Harbor, as well as ships that often ran ashore and collided with Dog Bar Reef. Though not a lighthouse itself, the Dog Bar Breakwater has been included in this chapter, as it is directly adjacent to the Eastern Point Lighthouse and because both sites are often photographed together due to their close proximity to one another.

Dog Bar Breakwater and Eastern Point Light, Gloucester, Mass.

THACHER ISLAND TWIN LIGHTS, 1905 (ABOVE), AND THE TWIN LIGHTS, 1907. Located on Thacher Island between Rockport and Gloucester, these lighthouses, popularly known as "the Twin Lights" or "Ann's Eyes," make up the Cape Ann Light Station, uniquely the only surviving multiple lighthouse station in the United States. Both built and first lit in 1771, the original lighthouses were the first to be built on Cape Ann. During the American Revolutionary War, local residents thought these lights were aiding the British, and townsfolk led by Dr. Samuel Rogers of Gloucester destroyed the lights for the American cause. They remained in ruins for the next several decades before they were reconstructed in 1861. As the 1861 (and present-day) lighthouses were built on the 1771 foundations, they are still considered the oldest established lighthouses in the area and are some of the oldest in Massachusetts and the United States as well.

THACHER'S NORTH LIGHT, 1907. The Thacher Island North Light is the oldest of the two original lighthouses on Thacher Island. Originally built in 1771, the tower was renovated along with its southern counterpart in 1861, when the present towers were built on the original foundations. The North Tower's light was removed in 1932 before being privately relit in 1989. It is currently maintained by the Town of Rockport.

Thatchers Northern Light, near Gloucester, Mass.

Thatchers Eastern Light, near Gloucester, Mass.

THACHER ISLAND EASTERN LIGHT, 1907. Officially named the Cape Ann Light and known as both the Thacher Island Southern and Eastern Light, this lighthouse was built in 1861 to its current state. Currently, though ownership of Thacher Island is split between the Town of Rockport and the US Fish and Wildlife Service, the US Coast Guard maintains the South Tower and a blinking red light there that was automated in 1979.

STRAITSMOUTH ISLAND LIGHTHOUSE, 1975 (ABOVE) AND 1918. Located on Straitsmouth Island, the first lighthouse on this station was built in 1835 at the entrance to Rockport Harbor and was rebuilt in 1851. Later, the lighthouse keeper's home was built on the island in 1878. By the 1890s, the lighthouse had fallen into disrepair, and the present lighthouse was built in 1896. The lighthouse, which is currently operated by the US Coast Guard, was automated in 1975. Additionally, once the lighthouse became automated, the original lighthouse keeper's home on the island fell into disrepair before eventually being renovated between 2015 and 2017. Though the lighthouse is maintained by the US Coast Guard, Straitsmouth Island itself is now owned by the Massachusetts Audubon Society and is operated as a bird sanctuary.

STRAITSMOUTH ISLAND AND LIGHT FROM THE ROCKS, ROCKPORT, MASS.

Two

HISTORIES AND FISHERIES
VIEWS OF GLOUCESTER

Gloucester is the largest city on Cape Ann and is the peninsula's main economic and cultural hub. Founded in 1623 by colonists from Dorchester, England, as the first European settlement in the Massachusetts Bay Colony, Gloucester's early years were marked by intense trials and tribulations. After the first attempt at a settlement failed due to various circumstances, the colonists ceased their plans to continue a settlement there and instead relocated to present-day Salem, Massachusetts (which was referred to as "Naumkeag" in the 1600s). This left the area mostly abandoned for the next approximately 15 years. However, almost two decades later, colonists again settled at Gloucester's present location, again attempting to establish a fishing operation there. Shortly after, as this settlement was successful on the second attempt, Gloucester was incorporated as a town in 1642. It quickly gained a reputation for a strong fishing industry (hence the nickname of "America's Oldest Seaport"), and as this industry developed, the town continued to grow.

By the 1800s, Gloucester had constructed numerous modern municipal buildings, storefronts, and residences and had become home to a large immigrant enclave. Incorporated as a city in 1873, Gloucester still continued to expand and additionally, at this time, became a major summertime tourist destination for various wealthy socialites, artists, and authors, who came to enjoy the area's natural charm. As a result, the tourism industry became just as vital to the city's survival as the maritime sector, and in Gloucester, numerous elegant summer resorts were constructed that brought a new clientele to the city. Additionally, this spurred the growth of many of Gloucester's neighborhoods, such as Magnolia and East Gloucester, which both became noted tourist destinations and resort areas in their own right and became home to art colonies that still have a presence today. Though Gloucester's resort and maritime industries dwindled in importance to the city's economic base in the ensuing years, the city has maintained its reputation for being an art haven, still boasts a summer tourist population, and continues to remain true to its maritime roots through annual celebrations and festivals dedicated to the city's heritage.

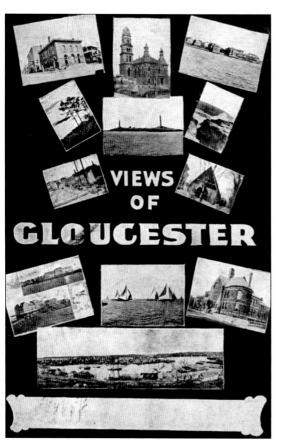

VIEWS OF GLOUCESTER, 1904. In the first two centuries following Gloucester's founding, toward the late 1800s and early 1900s, Gloucester had developed many architecturally appealing civic buildings and held numerous scenic sights and summer resorts that drew visitors to the area. As many visitors were drawn to the city's scenery, architecture, or summer maritime activities, this allowed Gloucester to capitalize on its newer and unique attractions and showcase them to tourists.

GLOUCESTER SIGHTS FROM HARBOR, 1906. Known for its panoramic views of Gloucester's fishing docks, downtown area, and coastline horizon overlooking the Atlantic Ocean, Gloucester Harbor allows sailors and passengers alike to see various sights such as the Ten Pound Island Lighthouse, the Eastern Point Lighthouse, and Norman's Woe while traveling in and out of the harbor as well as around Cape Ann's shores.

GLOUCESTER HARBOR, 1905. In addition to its available scenic views of the downtown area and the Atlantic Ocean, Gloucester Harbor is made up of numerous coves that house a diverse fleet of boats used by Gloucester residents and visitors, ranging from fishing vessels and small cargo boats to yachts as well as private watercraft. Additionally, the harbor is the site of many wharves that house local businesses and area attractions.

ROCKY NECK, GLOUCESTER, 1905. Known for being the site of one of the United States' oldest art colonies, Rocky Neck is a well-established neighborhood nestled between downtown Gloucester and Eastern Point on a peninsula inside Gloucester's Inner Harbor. The neighborhood began to gain prominence in the 1800s as a summer getaway for many influential artists and writers and has since become home to numerous eclectic galleries and businesses.

COVE EAST, GLOUCESTER, 1905. Located behind the Rocky Neck section of Gloucester along Gloucester's Inner Harbor, Cove East, also known as Smith Cove or Smith Cove Inlet, is home to numerous docks and fishing marinas. As the cove has water depths of over 14 feet, it is one of the most popular boat mooring areas of Gloucester Harbor for both small fishing vessels and private watercraft.

VINCENT COVE, GLOUCESTER, 1920. Though Gloucester Harbor has numerous coves and wharves that make up its seaport, Vincent Cove is a former important site in this harbor that no longer exists today. Known originally as "Vinson's Cove" for William Vinson, an early Gloucester settler, the area existed adjacent to Main Street and was used as a shipbuilding site. Additionally, several wharves operated there before the cove was filled in during the 1870s.

EAST GLOUCESTER WHARF, 1905. Much like the wharves one may immediately see in downtown Gloucester that are made up of fishing companies, whale watching operations, or other businesses and attractions, East Gloucester also held its own wharves in the Inner Harbor along Eastern Point and Rocky Neck that were often the homes of private docks and marinas.

WONSON'S COVE, 1940. Wonson's Cove (also known as "Wonson's Wharf") is a quaint cove located on East Gloucester. Its namesake derives from the locally noted Wonson family, who were prominent in East Gloucester. The Rocky Neck Beach is located along Wonson's Cove, and it also neighbors Rocky Neck Point, where the famous Tarr and Wonson Paint Factory is located.

A 6655 Main St., Gloucester, Mass.

MAIN STREET, GLOUCESTER, 1905 (ABOVE), AND MAIN STREET, GLOUCESTER, 1935. Located in downtown Gloucester toward Gloucester Harbor, Main Street is Gloucester's central hub and holds numerous storefronts, lofts, and apartment homes in charming brick and Colonial-style buildings off its roadway. Only walking distance to the wharves off Gloucester Harbor, Main Street was once the site of many fishing shops, pharmacies, a theater, and other miscellaneous enterprises, but in the past several decades, it has added many new storefronts, such as antiques outlets and gift shops. Furthermore, in recent years, Main Street has incorporated numerous eclectic restaurants, attractions, and boutiques that give the historic and charming roadway a youthful feel as well.

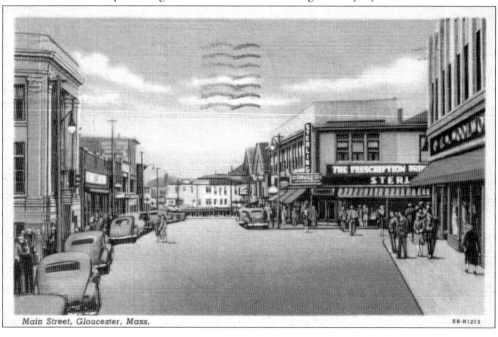

Main Street, Gloucester, Mass.

DALE AVENUE, 1905. Located in downtown Gloucester near Gloucester Harbor, Dale Avenue is known for holding some of Gloucester's oldest and most historic buildings, such as the first brick Gloucester High School, which was built in 1889; the Saunders House, which held the Sawyer Free Library; Gloucester's Great Depression–era post office, built in 1934; and other various Colonial-era homes and civic sites. Dale Avenue is also adorned with various statues and monuments that reference Gloucester's history. Additionally, Dale Avenue connects to several other roadways in downtown Gloucester, namely Middle and School Streets, and had remained relatively unchanged for the better part of a century. However, many of the buildings that adorned Dale Avenue have fallen victim to fire or alterations in the last several decades, leaving only an assortment of old buildings that used to be located in the vicinity.

STACY'S BOULEVARD, GLOUCESTER, MASS.

STACY BOULEVARD (ABOVE) AND THE BOULEVARD, BOTH GLOUCESTER, 1945. Stacy Boulevard is located in Gloucester's downtown area and gives immaculate views of the Atlantic Ocean, Ten Pound Island, and both the eastern and western sides of Gloucester Harbor. Stretching roughly half a mile, the boulevard is home to several of Gloucester's most famous and culturally important sites, such as the Gloucester Fishermen's Memorial Statue and the Fishermen's Wives Memorial Statue. Additionally, the boulevard is adorned with numerous Colonial-era homes along the roadway and is home to a long walkway that borders the Atlantic Ocean behind a railed seawall. Furthermore, the boulevard leads one past the Blynman Bridge and Stage Fort Park before bringing them toward mainland Essex County.

THE BOULEVARD
GLOUCESTER. MASS.

9-2143

WESTERN AVENUE, GLOUCESTER, 1945 (ABOVE), AND WESTERN AVENUE, GLOUCESTER, 1920. Gloucester's scenic Western Avenue is located past the Blynman Bridge and Stage Fort Park and is a several-mile-long roadway that brings one from downtown Gloucester and the Freshwater Cove area to the community of Magnolia. The roadway was once unpaved and was used by horse riders. The construction of the Blynman Bridge in the 1920s spurred the creation of the paved Western Avenue, which allowed for better and easier transportation between Magnolia, where many summer tourists lodged, and the attractions of downtown Gloucester. Additionally, though known for allowing easier transportation and vehicle travel across Cape Ann, several local natural sites, including Rafe's Chasm Park, are located off Western Avenue as well.

WESTERN AVENUE, GLOUCESTER, MASS.

Old Man of "Joppa," Gloucester, Mass.

THE OLD MAN OF JOPPA, 1915 (ABOVE), AND THE OLD JOPPA ROAD, 1920. Joppa was a small farming community that existed between the 18th and 20th centuries and was once the only farming area between Gloucester and Rockport. The rural area sat in a marshy and rocky region of the peninsula and was home to many early settlers in the Cape Ann region whose families became prominent in the vicinity, including Hannah Jumper, who became a noted temperance advocate in the region in the 1800s. However, though it was known as a popular farming area, the population in this community remained low, and as Gloucester continued to expand in the 1800s with the onset of new immigrants to the region and the growing tourism industry, much of the land in Joppa was bought and developed.

SOUVENIR OF GLOUCESTER, 1907 (ABOVE), AND GLOUCESTER CITY HALL, 1905. Located on Dale Avenue in Gloucester, Gloucester City Hall was built in 1870 (though some sources claim it was built in 1869) and was dedicated in 1871. This building was also used as the center of Gloucester's municipal offices when it was formally incorporated as a city in 1873. Furthermore, this brick, two-story building is known for its unique pyramidal roof and cupolas and has housed offices for city departments and politicians since its creation. Though it has undergone several interior renovations in past decades, Gloucester City Hall is still in use today after more than 150 years of operation and was placed in the National Register of Historic Places in 1973, becoming one of many buildings in Gloucester to earn that designation.

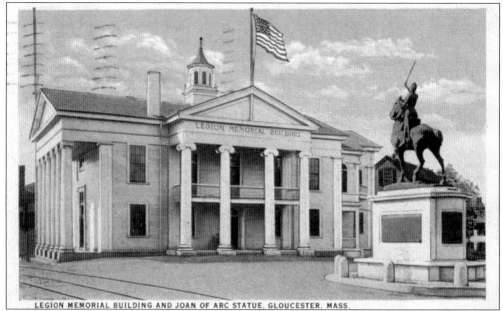

LEGION MEMORIAL BUILDING AND JOAN OF ARC STATUE, GLOUCESTER, MASS.

LEGION BUILDING AND STATUE, 1920. This building, constructed in 1801, acted as Gloucester's first town hall. It was eventually occupied by the private Forbes School from 1867 to 1917 and later leased by Gloucester's chapter of the American Legion in 1920. Additionally, the *Joan of Arc* statue (Gloucester's World War I memorial statue), sculpted by Anna Hyatt Huntington, was erected outside of the building in 1918 to honor Gloucester soldiers who served in that conflict.

THE ELKS REST, BEACHBROOK CEMETERY, WEST GLOUCESTER, MASS.

BEECHBROOK CEMETERY AND ELKS STATUE, 1920. Founded in 1878 and owned by the City of Gloucester, Beechbrook Cemetery was the first public cemetery located in West Gloucester and was the second city cemetery made in the municipality. This cemetery is the largest in Gloucester and holds numerous memorials in honor of Gloucester's fishermen, as well as the Elks Rest Statue, which was made in 1904 in honor of Gloucester's deceased Elks Lodge members.

GLOUCESTER POST OFFICE AND CUSTOMS HOUSE, 1905. The US Customs House was established in Gloucester in 1789, and the first Gloucester Post Office was built thereafter in 1792. This building was constructed in the early 1800s and housed both the post office and US Customs House, which shared the space. Eventually, the Gloucester Customs House was decommissioned from the building in 1908, and the post office was moved in 1932.

GLOUCESTER POST OFFICE, 1935. The second Gloucester Post Office was built with funds from the New Deal program. Construction on the building began in 1932 and concluded in 1934, though some claim it was completed in early 1935. Still, this more modern post office replaced the smaller brick post office and is currently in use today.

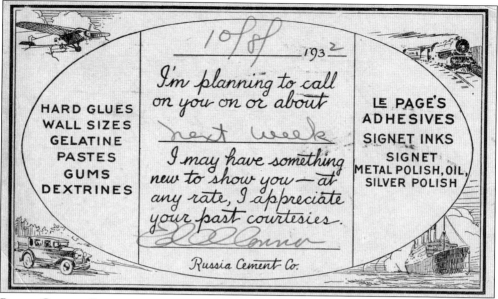

HARD GLUES
WALL SIZES
GELATINE
PASTES
GUMS
DEXTRINES

10/8/ 193²

I'm planning to call on you on or about next week I may have something new to show you — at any rate, I appreciate your past courtesies.

Russia Cement Co.

LE PAGE'S
ADHESIVES
SIGNET INKS
SIGNET
METAL POLISH, OIL,
SILVER POLISH

RUSSIA CEMENT COMPANY AND LEPAGE'S FACTORY, 1932. LePage's Glue was a product of the Russia Cement Company, a construction business that operated in the Northern United States. In 1842, the Russia Cement Company began operations in Gloucester, where LePage's products were produced. In 1887, LePage's began operating in a factory built in 1861 along the Annisquam River. The factory operated there until it closed in 2001. The building was then sold and eventually became an apartment complex.

FRANK E. DAVIS COMPANY BUILDING, 1920. Also known as the Davis Brothers Fisheries, the Frank E. Davis Fish Company was founded in 1885 and held operations in a building located on Gloucester's Central Wharf. The company was a major fishing business in the Cape Ann region and was also a well-known regional fishing business until it closed down in 1959.

US FISH HATCHERY, GLOUCESTER, 1905. Located on Ten Pound Island, Gloucester's US Fish Hatchery was a wooden building constructed in 1889 with funds from the federal government. It was built to replenish fish populations on Cape Ann after reports of overfishing had arisen. Eventually, it was abandoned in 1954 when the Ten Pound Island Light Station was decommissioned. By the time preservationists purchased the island in 1989, the hatchery was irreparable, and it was demolished.

GLOUCESTER, MASS. ARMORY

NATIONAL GUARD ARMORY, GLOUCESTER, 1906. The Gloucester National Guard Armory was located on Prospect Street, served as a recruitment station for soldiers during various wars, and provided weapons and supplies to soldiers and National Guard members in the area. The building was renovated in the 1930s with funds from the New Deal program before it was decommissioned as an armory and turned into senior housing in 1986, which is how it stands today.

YMCA BUILDING, GLOUCESTER, 1906. Gloucester's chapter of the Young Men's Christian Association began in 1858 when the YMCA leased the second floor of Gloucester's bank. Eventually, in the late 1800s to early 1900s, a permanent building was constructed for the YMCA, which is seen in this World War I postcard that offered membership to veterans of that conflict. This building housed the chapter until 1973.

ADDISON GILBERT HOSPITAL, GLOUCESTER, 1906. Founded in 1889, the Addison Gilbert Hospital was named for Addison Gilbert, a Gloucester philanthropist and politician who gave money for its establishment. The hospital was the first public hospital on Cape Ann and provided essential care for residents in the area, who were rather isolated from the rest of Essex County. The hospital has also expanded from holding operations in one brick building to now consisting of several units.

SAWYER FREE LIBRARY, 1905. The Sawyer Free Library was officially established in 1872 with the help of Gloucester businessman Samuel Sawyer, the library's namesake, who gave numerous gifts to the former Gloucester Lyceum to help establish a public library. Later, in 1884, Sawyer bought a 1764-built home in Gloucester that housed the library for over a century. Though this building was expanded, the library outgrew it and moved into its current facility in 1976.

CAPE ANN SCIENTIFIC AND LITERARY ASSOCIATION, 1930. Founded in 1875, the Cape Ann Scientific and Literary Association was created by local intellectuals to collect and preserve items of Cape Ann's culture and history and promote academic education to the Cape Ann public. The organization first gained its permanent residence at the Captain Elias Davis House in the early 1920s and structurally grew over the succeeding decades before being formally renamed the Cape Ann Museum in 2007.

GLOUCESTER HIGH SCHOOL, DALE AVENUE, 1905. The Gloucester High School was first established in 1839 in a one-room schoolhouse. In 1851, it was moved into a new schoolhouse that eventually burned down in 1887. In 1889, a new brick high school on Dale Avenue opened, and it operated until 1939, when the high school moved to its current location. This building was then made the Central Grammar School in 1940, but it eventually became senior housing.

Gloucester High School, Gloucester, Mass.

GLOUCESTER HIGH SCHOOL, 1945. In the decades following the opening of the Gloucester High School on Dale Avenue in 1889, Gloucester's population continued to increase with the influx of immigrants and newcomers. By the 1930s, the need for a new schoolhouse was evident, and construction began on a three-story schoolhouse in Gloucester in 1937. It opened in 1939 on Leslie O. Johnson Road and still operates as the current Gloucester High School.

Blyman Bridge (Cut Bridge) Gloucester, Mass.   7B273-N

BLYNMAN BRIDGE, GLOUCESTER, 1945. Built in 1907, the Blynman Bridge, also known as the "cut bridge," was created to provide a driving route over the Blynman Canal in Gloucester. Previously, Cape Ann residents had to travel across the canal to mainland Essex County by ferry. This bridge was therefore essential for better transportation and was paved in 1920 to accommodate automobile travel. It has been renovated several times and is still in use today.

A. PIATT ANDREW BRIDGE, 1953. Completed in 1950, the A. Piatt Andrew Bridge was the first modern bridge crossing the Annisquam River to be built on Cape Ann and is credited with aiding in Gloucester's transformation from a small town to a bustling city, as it allowed more traffic into the area. Prior to its construction, the Blynman Bridge was the only bridge that allowed Gloucester and Rockport residents to enter and leave the island.

GLOUCESTER RAIL DEPOT, 1905. Built in 1847, the Gloucester Railroad Depot was originally served by the Eastern Railroad, which ran daily trains from Boston, Massachusetts, to Ellsworth, Maine, and was later operated under the Boston & Maine Railroad. This particular building operated as Gloucester's train depot until 2005, when a new, modern station was built to serve the community.

MASSACHUSETTS BAY TRANSIT AUTHORITY TRAIN, GLOUCESTER, 1988. In 1964, the Massachusetts Bay Transit Authority (MBTA) was established, and it took control of the lines held by the Boston & Maine Railroad in 1965. However, due to funding disputes between the MBTA and local municipalities, many lines between Essex County towns were discontinued. By the late 1960s, most lines were restored, and the MBTA continues to operate trains in and out of the Gloucester Depot in the present day.

OLD RIGGS HOUSE, GLOUCESTER, 1910. Built in the 1640s, the Ancient Riggs House, Cape Ann's oldest home, is one of the last surviving squared-log-style homes in Massachusetts. Originally owned by Thomas Riggs, Gloucester's first schoolmaster and town clerk, it remained in the Riggs family until recent decades. After the home's 1990s sale, running water and modern electricity were added to it in 1998, and it was operated as an inn until 2021.

OLD WHEELER HOUSE, WHEELER POINT, GLOUCESTER, MASS.

OLD WHEELER HOUSE, 1920S. Constructed in approximately 1720, the Dyke-Wheeler House was built by Richard Dyke and was expanded in roughly 1800 by later owners. The home was thought to have been built in the 1600s until further research proved its 18th-century origins. The residence, located on Wheeler's Point in Gloucester, was owned for many years by the Wheeler family, for whom Wheeler's Point is named. It is currently in private ownership.

OLD ELLERY HOUSE, 1920 (ABOVE), AND OLD ELLERY HOUSE, BOTH GLOUCESTER, 1905. Built in 1710 in the former Gloucester Town Green and currently known as the White-Ellery House, this building is one of several surviving 18th-century homes in the region. Besides its age, the house is known for its unique architectural elements, including its saltbox frame and relatively untouched 1700s-era interior design. Additionally, its preservation story has gained it further notoriety; in 1947, while the house was owned by the Ellery family of Gloucester, the Route 128 Rotary was designed, and plans for its construction went underway. As the rotary's construction would have threatened the house, the City of Gloucester took ownership of the home that year under eminent domain, and it was then sold to what is now the Cape Ann Museum (which still owns it). To protect it from the rotary construction, the museum then moved the home 100 yards, where it remains today.

THE OLD BABSON HOMESTEAD, 1920. The Babson-Alling House, built by William Allen in 1740, is a sophisticated home located in Gloucester's former town center. The house has been remodeled several times. Eventually, threats to its safety from the construction of the Route 128 Rotary in the 1940s forced protective fences to be placed around it. It has remained like that since and was privately owned before the Cape Ann Museum purchased it in 2019.

MURRAY GILMAN HOUSE, GLOUCESTER, MASS.

MURRAY GILMAN HOUSE, 1920. The Sargent Murray Gilman House, built in 1782, was first owned by Judith Sargent Murray, a philosopher and women's rights advocate who was also the wife of Rev. John Murray, the founder of the Unitarian Universalist church denomination. The house was also the residence of local leaders in both Gloucester's community and Gloucester's maritime industry before preservationists bought the home and established it as the Sargent House Museum in 1919.

The Hermitage, Gloucester, Mass.

THE HERMITAGE, GLOUCESTER, 1920. The Hermitage was a quaint cabin home in the Ravenswood section of Gloucester that belonged to Mason Walton, a dedicated nature observer who wrote for *Field and Stream* magazine under the name "the Hermit." Walton died in 1917, and a plaque commemorating his life and his cabin was erected by the Gloucester Women's Club in 1933. Though Walton's cabin burned down in 1948, the plaque is still in existence.

Cottages, Bass Rocks, Gloucester, Mass.

COTTAGES AT BASS ROCKS, 1912. Though many of Gloucester's historic homes can be found in the former Town Green area or the present downtown, the Bass Rocks section of Gloucester is known for being the site of many elegant homes and summer resorts, too. Furthermore, the Bass Rocks area holds numerous picturesque summer cottages built with Colonial-era architectural themes, such as the Sherman Cottage, a popular home often featured in paintings of the Gloucester seashore.

3. THE UNIVERSALIST CHURCH, BUILT 1806, GLOUCESTER, MASS.

THE FIRST UNIVERSALIST CHURCH, GLOUCESTER, 1920. Though its congregation was first founded in 1779 as the Independent Christian Church, the Gloucester Unitarian Universalist Church was built in 1806 and was the first Unitarian church established in the United States. Located on Church Street in Gloucester, this church has stood the same since it was built but has undergone several renovations. Though the only active Unitarian church in Gloucester in the present day, it used to be one of two Unitarian congregations in Gloucester; the other Unitarian church, the former First Parish Church on Middle Street, was created in 1828 and closed by 1950. At that time, the church was bought and it became home to the Temple Ahavat Achim synagogue before it burned down in 2007. The Gloucester Unitarian Universalist Church remains the last surviving original 1800s-era Unitarian church building that was constructed in the city.

HARBOR METHODIST CHURCH, GLOUCESTER, 1905. The Harbor Methodist Church was the first Methodist church built in Gloucester and was located on Prospect Street. Built in 1828, it was known as the "church on the rock" and allowed Methodists in Gloucester a place to worship in the town's early years. This church remained popular even after the 1838 formation of the Riverdale Methodist Meetinghouse, which saw the majority of Cape Ann Methodists attend instead. Eventually, this church was placed for sale in 1858 after the congregation moved, and the building was purchased by preservationists in 1859. Its use after its purchase by preservationists is unknown for certain, but it stood until shortly after the turn of the 20th century. After this building was decommissioned as a church, the Riverdale Methodist Meetinghouse (also known as the Riverdale Methodist Church and Gloucester Methodist Church) became Gloucester's lone Methodist church.

ST. JOHN'S PROTESTANT EPISCOPAL CHURCH (RIGHT) AND ST. JOHN'S EPISCOPAL CHURCH, BOTH GLOUCESTER, 1910. Initially named St. John's Church, this congregation was founded in 1863 under Rev. Joshua Pierce and was named for Reverend Pierce's home congregation in Portsmouth, New Hampshire. The church building was completed in 1864 on land donated by the church's first benefactor, Theron Johnson Dale, a summer resident of Gloucester. After his death in 1871, it was discovered that he had paid for the land the church sat on in full, allowing the church to maintain full ownership of the building and land by the time it was consecrated in 1874. In its early years, the church was largely aligned with Anglican fishermen who worshiped here, but it eventually began to cater to wealthier Episcopalian tourists who spent summers in Gloucester. Furthermore, the church was noted for also helping establish the Gloucester Fishermen's Institute, an organization that aided impoverished fishermen.

St. John's Protestant Episcopal Church, Gloucester, Mass.

St. John's Episcopal Church, Gloucester, Mass.

"OUR LADY OF GOOD VOYAGE CHURCH"
GLOUCESTER, MASS.

PUBLISHED BY EDWIN C. MCINTIRE, GLOUCESTER, MASS.

FIRST GOOD VOYAGE CATHOLIC CHURCH, 1910 (LEFT), AND SECOND GOOD VOYAGE CATHOLIC CHURCH, GLOUCESTER, 1920.
By 1888, Gloucester held the nation's largest Portuguese enclave, and as many Portuguese immigrants moved to Gloucester, the need for a church that represented their beliefs became evident. Built in 1893, Our Lady of Good Voyage Catholic Church was established as the first Portuguese Catholic church in Gloucester. The original church burned down in 1914 and was replaced by its current church structure that year. Presently, the church is the only Mission-style church in Gloucester and is modeled after Catholic churches in the Azores. Additionally, many of the Portuguese immigrants in Gloucester worked in the maritime industry, which served as the inspiration behind the church's mission to worship saints who protected fishermen, a tradition practiced among Catholics in the Azores as well.

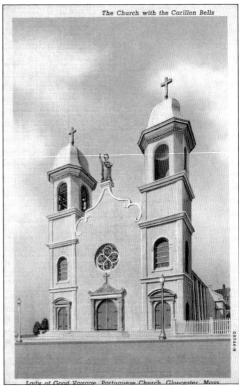

The Church with the Carillon Bells

Lady of Good Voyage Portuguese Church Gloucester Mass

OUR LADY OF GOOD VOYAGE STATUE, 1960. As Our Lady of Good Voyage Catholic Church is deeply rooted in maritime culture, the church holds a statue named *Our Lady* that honors the biblical Madonna, who is said to watch over fishermen and their families. Catholic Portuguese fishermen in the Azores also worshiped the Madonna for this reason, and this sentiment was carried on when this church was founded by Portuguese immigrants and their families in Gloucester.

SHRINE OF THE FISHERMAN, 1970. The importance of worshiping saints who protect fishermen at sea is a sentiment in Gloucester's Italian Catholic community as well. The statue of St. Peter was made in 1926 and is held at the St. Peter's Club in Gloucester. The statue is also carried annually on a float at a local festival referred to as "GreasyPole," which celebrates Gloucester's cultural heritage.

St. Ann's Catholic Church, 1920.

St. Ann's Catholic Church was established in 1855 to accommodate the small population of Catholics on Cape Ann at that time. The church was first established in the old Baptist Church of Gloucester, which was moved to Pleasant Street in 1855 when the congregation was established. Eventually, the congregation outgrew that building and moved to this stone church, built in 1876, which is still used by the congregation today.

St. Peter's Catholic Church, 1920.

St. Peter's Catholic Church of Gloucester was built in approximately 1900 and was dedicated to St. Peter, who is believed to protect fishermen at sea. Similar to other Catholic churches in Gloucester, this maritime sentiment was an important part of the congregation's beliefs until the church closed in the early 2000s. After the church closed, the church building was sold and converted to private residences.

15. ST. ANN'S CHURCH, GLOUCESTER, MASS.

ST. PETER'S CHURCH, GLOUCESTER, MASS.

Three

From Annisquam to Magnolia
Gloucester's Neighborhoods

Along with being the site of a bustling downtown and a well-known harbor, Gloucester is made up of numerous residential hamlets that span across the Cape Ann peninsula. Aside from Gloucester's general history and culture, these neighborhoods and communities have their own unique histories and identities that have contributed to Cape Ann's heritage as well. Three of these communities that are notably featured in this book are Annisquam, Lanesville, and Magnolia. To briefly discuss each of these communities, Annisquam is a village noted for its own maritime history that is located on western Cape Ann bordering the town of Essex. The Annisquam vicinity was also the site of Dogtown. An abandoned community that existed during Cape Ann's earlier days, Dogtown is now the site of the Riverdale section of Gloucester (which is also in the Annisquam area). Though Annisquam itself was known for its former elite ties and separate culture aside from Gloucester, it too gained wealth and prosperity from the maritime industry, and many symbols from this past still exist in that community, such as the Annisquam Lighthouse and the Annisquam Yacht Club. This is similar to Lanesville, located at the northern tip of Cape Ann near Rockport, which was, at one point, a famed granite-producing community that held a successful fishing harbor.

Though Annisquam and Lanesville are known for their maritime pasts, Magnolia, located on the southern end of Gloucester on the city's border with Manchester-by-the-Sea, is a community known for its contributions to Cape Ann's notoriety as a summer vacation destination as well as for its former upscale environment. Magnolia held several summer resorts, such as the Oceanside and the Hesperus, that drew tourists from larger Northern cities, such as Boston and New York City. It was also home to many high-end boutiques and attractions that later became frequented by famous celebrities and politicians as well, thus contributing to Gloucester and Cape Ann's hospitality and tourism industry. Overall, as Gloucester and Cape Ann's many neighborhoods and communities contribute to its unique and diverse history for an array of reasons, these communities' own characteristics and histories are captured in this chapter to celebrate their individual stories.

River Scene, Annisquam, Mass.

ANNISQUAM RIVER, 1906 (ABOVE), AND ANNISQUAM HARBOR, 1945. Technically an estuary, the Annisquam River runs four miles across the western side of Cape Ann, separating the island peninsula from the rest of mainland Essex County, Massachusetts. The river has been vital for the community's success, serving as a fruitful fishing and trading site. Notably, located along the Annisquam River is the village of Annisquam, founded in 1631, which is known for its background within Cape Ann's granite industry and its own eclectic fine arts history. Also, Wigwam Point, located at the tip of the Annisquam community's peninsula, is the home of Annisquam Lighthouse, an essential beacon for sailors and fishermen traveling the Cape Ann region. Additionally, near the village of Annisquam is Annisquam Harbor, a former major shipbuilding production center and fishing port that was once a rival to Gloucester Harbor.

ANNISQUAM HARBOR
ANNISQUAM, MASS.

Annisquam Bridge, showing Annisquam, Mass.

30169

ANNISQUAM BRIDGE, 1906. Built over Lobster Cove, the Annisquam Bridge was first constructed in 1847 before its current, woodpile-style bridge was built in 1861. It is still in existence after undergoing several renovations and overhauls, including a complete reconstruction between 1946 and 1947. The Annisquam Bridge closed to vehicles in 1968 and is now a pedestrian-only bridge.

YACHT CLUB, ANNISQUAM, MASS.

ANNISQUAM YACHT CLUB. Established in 1896, the Annisquam Yacht Club is situated on the Annisquam River and is roughly half a mile from the Annisquam Lighthouse. Founded and maintained as a private club since its inception, along with holding a popular tennis court, the club is popular among tourists and locals of Cape Ann who enjoy sailing and yachting.

ANNISQUAM WILLOWS, 1906 (ABOVE), AND ANNISQUAM WILLOWS ROAD, 1904. There was a push to make a roadway in the Annisquam neighborhood in the 1840s, but citizens had difficulties constructing one because of the swampy and marshy landscape the village sat in. To alleviate this issue, citizens purchased willow trees that would absorb excess water and create a stable foundation for a road to be constructed on. The Annisquam willows were planted in 1847 and grew beautifully over the next several decades along present-day Washington Street before a blight infected the plants in the 1950s and killed most of them. Several willow trees remain in the area, but they are in various scattered locations.

THE WHALE'S JAW, DOGTOWN COMMON, 1907 (ABOVE) AND 1920. "The Whale's Jaw" is the name given to one of the many natural boulders that line the old Dogtown Commons area. The Whale's Jaw was the largest of these boulders but suffered a partial collapse in 1989 when a brush fire overheated the rock structure. Dogtown Commons, the site of the abandoned Dogtown community of Gloucester that existed near present-day Annisquam and Riverdale, additionally features over 30 other rocks known as "Babson Boulders." These rocks got their name from the inspirational messages carved on them that were commissioned by Roger Babson, an influential Gloucester native. The project of carving the messages on them itself was carried out by Works Progress Administration laborers during the Great Depression. Presently, these boulders, and the Whale's Jaw rock, are all scattered in a forested area accessible by trails.

Landing Fish, Lanesville, Mass.

LANDING FISH, LANESVILLE, 1905.
Settled in the late 1600s as a small village on the northern tip of Cape Ann, Lanesville became a significant regional fishing center by the early 1800s that rivaled nearby Rockport. Though rather small compared to Gloucester, Lanesville's harbor still saw abundant yields of fish caught in local waters, allowing the community to gain prosperity and notoriety from this industry.

FISH HOUSES AT LANESVILLE HARBOR, 1920. Lanesville became a popular fishing center in the early 1800s, spurring the construction of many fishing shacks and houses along the Lanesville Harbor. However, though Lanesville was known for its fishing industry, the community's harbor became popular for shipping and transporting locally sourced granite rocks by the mid-1800s, marking a shift in the community's status from a fishing village to a commercial center as well.

FISH HOUSES, LANESVILLE HARBOR, GLOUCESTER, MASS.

Coggeshall Camp from Shore Front, Lanesville, Mass.

CAMP COGGESHALL, LANESVILLE, 1910. The Coggeshall Camp of Lanesville was established in approximately 1906 by John Coggeshall, an artist from Fall River, Massachusetts, who was known for his photography work and paintings. Although Coggeshall was a resident of Lowell, he operated his camp in Lanesville until his demise. At this camp, which was often operated in the summer months when tourists and visitors vacationed on Cape Ann, classes were held for both beginners and advanced students who came here to learn from an acclaimed artist. Coggeshall's most noted classes included lessons in drawing, oil painting, and watercolor painting. The camp let students board as well, which allowed people from various places to visit and attend classes while enjoying the local scenery. Eventually, with over 20 years of operation, the camp closed in 1928 after Coggeshall's death, and it was bought and sold numerous times. Though most of the camp has been demolished over time, some buildings remain intact today under private ownership.

Sacred Heart Church - Lanesville, Cape Ann, Mass.

SACRED HEART CHURCH, LANESVILLE, 1910. Constructed between Lanesville and the Bay View neighborhood of Gloucester in 1876, the Sacred Heart Church was the first permanent Catholic church built in Lanesville, even though mass had been celebrated in the community since 1850 in the village hall. It was one of two major churches in the Lanesville community, the other being Lanesville Orthodox Congregational Church, which served Protestant residents. Furthermore, Sacred Heart Church provided Catholic religious education to congregation members beginning in 1855, when Sunday school was established in the church. Sunday school continued to be held until the church eventually closed its doors. After serving the Lanesville community for over a century and a half, the Sacred Heart Church was decommissioned in 2005 and was placed for sale in 2006. It was purchased privately the year it was listed and is now in private ownership.

FOLLY COVE, LANESVILLE, 1910. Initially settled as its own community in the early 1700s, Folly Cove began as a small, sparsely populated fishing and farming village, and it maintained this status for the first century of its existence. By the mid-1800s, the local granite industry became the leading industry in the community, which led more immigrants to settle in Folly Cove and expand the community's population and boundaries, eventually merging it into Lanesville.

PLUM COVE BEACH, LANESVILLE, 1910. One of the Lanesville community's most popular recreation spots, Plum Cove Beach is a crescent-shaped beach surrounded by picturesque rocky cliffs and trees. Currently operated as a free public beach, Plum Cove Beach is frequented by families, as well as those who enjoy activities such as fishing, swimming, or snorkeling.

7588. WEST FROM THE NEW MAGNOLIA, MAGNOLIA, MASS.

GENERAL VIEW OF MAGNOLIA, 1904. Magnolia is a seaside community in southern Gloucester, located on the border of Gloucester and Manchester-by-the-Sea. Historically, Magnolia has been known for its luxurious summer resorts that hosted wealthy tourists from larger cities. It first gained this reputation after the Civil War, when socialites from Boston and its surrounding areas would visit in the warmer months. The community grew, and by the 1890s, Magnolia was home to the Hesperus, the Oceanside, and the New Magnolia, all of which contributed to the area's status as a luxurious retreat for wealthy vacationers. Magnolia was also home to mansions and numerous upscale stores that entertained tourists. However, in the succeeding decades, the resorts in Magnolia either burned down or closed, and the community's reputation as an upscale retreat began to recede. Nevertheless, although Magnolia's hospitality heyday is in the past, the community has maintained its quaint and charming reputation.

The Magnolia Road,
between Magnolia and Gloucester, Mass.

THE MAGNOLIA ROAD, 1906. Currently the site of Western Avenue, this stretch of road existed past "the cut," another name for the canal that separates Gloucester and mainland Essex County. Prior to the development of paved roads for automobiles, this dirt road was the route to Magnolia from downtown Gloucester and allowed citizens to travel between the two communities on horseback.

7585. BATHING BEACH, MAGNOLIA, MASS.

THE BATHING BEACH, MAGNOLIA, 1904. Magnolia's seasonal tourists came from areas abroad due to its quaint seaside charm and desirable summer weather, which made visiting beaches a popular activity. Most of the area's public beaches were located in Gloucester, while many of Magnolia's popular bathing beaches were located alongside beachside resorts and were privately operated by the high-end resorts in the community.

THE ARCADE, LEXINGTON AVE., MAGNOLIA, MASS.

THE ARCADE, MAGNOLIA, 1904. Built in the late 1800s, the Arcade in Magnolia operated on Lexington Avenue and was a gathering place for tourist socialites. The business operated for a brief period before becoming home to Hodgson, Kennard, and Company, an upscale retail store. Eventually, that business closed, and the building became home to several other enterprises before being renovated in recent decades. Though altered, it is still standing today.

10657. RAILROAD STATION, MAGNOLIA, MASS.

MAGNOLIA RAIL DEPOT, 1906. The Magnolia Rail Depot was technically formerly located on Magnolia Avenue in Manchester-by-the-Sea, near the southern end of the Magnolia community. Built in the late 1800s, it was established to allow wealthy visitors from large cities the opportunity to more easily travel to and from Magnolia's large resorts in the summer months. Closed during winter, it remained open for nearly 60 years until it was demolished in the mid-20th century.

The Men's Club House, Magnolia, Mass.

MEN'S CLUB HOUSE, MAGNOLIA, 1913. Known as the Men's Club House of Magnolia, this building, though not believed to be in existence in the present day, served as the site of a former Masonic lodge in the community. These Masonic groups, also commonly known as Freemasons' clubs, are organizations whose membership is offered exclusively to men and whose members often undertake volunteer work or charitable projects.

R 7138 The Library, Magnolia, Mass

THE LIBRARY, MAGNOLIA, 1907. Established in 1886, the Magnolia Library and Community Center was built on Norman Avenue, and though exteriorly altered, it has remained in its original building since its inception. Currently, the library has expanded beyond providing books to the community and is presently a place of gathering for members of the Magnolia community, as well as a voting place and venue for town hall meetings.

UNION CONGREGATIONAL CHURCH, MAGNOLIA, 1928. Union Congregational Church was built in Magnolia in roughly 1922 and was established due to the growing Protestant population in the community, who also frequented both the Episcopal church in Magnolia and the local Methodist churches. Though other churches in Magnolia have closed, the Union Congregational Church is still open in the present day.

ST. JOSEPH'S CATHOLIC CHURCH, MAGNOLIA, 1914. St. Joseph's Catholic Church was constructed in 1911 and was built with stones from various Magnolia properties. It was a place of gathering and community for Magnolia's Catholic residents and operated for nearly a century before it closed in 2005. It was demolished in 2008, and at the time of its demolition, artifacts from the building were saved and rehomed to other nearby churches, allowing its legacy to continue.

THE HAMMOND MUSEUM, 1965. The Hammond Castle, constructed along the Magnolia coastline, was built between 1926 and 1929. It was designed by John Hays Hammond Jr., a famed American inventor. The castle, built with Medieval, Gothic, and Renaissance inspirations, was Hammond's laboratory and held his large personal collection of artifacts from Roman antiquity to the Renaissance era. Soon after the castle was completed in 1929, it was opened as a museum in 1930.

THE HAMMOND MUSEUM INTERIOR, 1939. As the Hammond Castle Museum was created with architectural inspirations from the Renaissance and Medieval periods, many original artifacts from these periods (as well as replicas) are housed inside the museum. These items had been part of John Hays Hammond's personal collection of artifacts and also notably include items from Roman antiquity.

RAFE'S CHASM, MAGNOLIA, MASS.

RAFE'S CHASM, MAGNOLIA, 1904.
One of Gloucester's most noted natural sites is a large rock fissure located along the Atlantic Ocean in Magnolia, which became known as Rafe's Chasm beginning in the 1850s. Though located on private land, the rock itself is surrounded by Rafe's Chasm Park, a recreational area sold to the City of Gloucester in 1959.

NORMAN'S WOE, MAGNOLIA, 1905. In addition to Rafe's Chasm, another one of Gloucester's natural sites located in the vicinity of the Magnolia community is Norman's Woe, a large rock reef that sits in western Gloucester Harbor. Though known for its natural beauty, the rock has been the cause of several shipwrecks and is also the subject of Henry Wadsworth Longfellow's fictitious poem "The Wreck of the Hesperus."

Photo. Only. Copyright 1905 by the Rotograph Co.
G 7135 "Norman's Woe", Magnolia, Mass.

Four

Luxury and Leisure
Tourism and Recreation
on Cape Ann

The Cape Ann peninsula has long been known for its beautiful, picturesque beaches and natural landscape that draw many to the region during warmer months, when its scenery can be most appreciated. Though the area's beauty had long been realized by its indigenous forebears and early colonists, in the mid-1800s, when Cape Ann' population began to grow significantly, numerous resorts and hotels were developed to capitalize on the landscape and scenery and draw tourists vacationing in New England. These resorts and hotels made both Gloucester and the Cape Ann peninsula in general hotspots for summer recreation and hospitality during the next century to come. These resorts and hotels were often large in size with grand decor and interior elements and were known to feature recreational, sporting, and leisure activities, which especially catered to wealthy tourists visiting the area and soon gave Cape Ann a reputation for upscale lodging and tourism opportunities.

Though several smaller hotels were formed in the early 1840s (such as the Fairview Inn), the first of the luxurious resorts was the Pavilion Hotel, built in 1849, which paved the way for the dozens of resorts that would be formed by the late 1800s and the early 1900s. These hotels were not limited solely to Gloucester; resorts began being constructed in smaller towns and hamlets, such as Rockport and the Magnolia community of Gloucester, which brought clientele suited to the arts and upscale sectors to these places as well. Additionally, some of Cape Ann's most recognizable hotels and resorts, such as the Oceanside in Magnolia, drew celebrities and elite clients to the area and helped contribute to Cape Ann's transformation from a small, sleepy seaside peninsula into one of the nation's most popular summer destinations.

However, though the tourism sector was immensely important to Gloucester and Cape Ann's economies, these resorts and hotels eventually became less popular with the onset of the Great Depression, leading to a decline in this industry. Many of these resorts had closed by this time, but throughout the ensuing decades, there were numerous fires that destroyed several of the remaining resorts, such as the Oceanside and (most of) the Moorland Complex, signaling the end of Cape Ann's tourism heyday by the latter end of the 20th century. Though the hotels and resorts of Cape Ann's past are largely gone, the peninsula's beaches, parks (such as Stage Fort Park), and recreational sites still draw visitors to the region and remain popular among locals as well.

Straitsmouth Inn
Rockport, Mass.

STRAITSMOUTH INN, 1905. The Straitsmouth Inn was built in 1906 on Straitsmouth Island, off the coast of Rockport, which is also the location of the Straitsmouth Island Lighthouse. Notably, while in operation, this hotel was only accessible by ferry. It was mostly destroyed after catching fire in 1958. Currently, one part of this former hotel that survived the 1958 blaze continues to operate as the Seafarer Inn.

TURK'S HEAD INN, ROCKPORT, MASS.

THE TURK'S HEAD INN, 1910. Known as one of the most elegant hotels on Cape Ann, the Turk's Head Inn was located in southern Rockport. First built around the turn of the 20th century, with the newer section being built around 1905, the Turk's Head Inn was known for its views of the Thacher Island Lighthouses and Loblolly Cove. Eventually, the hotel closed in 1965, and fires in 1968 and 1970 led to its demolition.

The Fairview, East Gloucester, Mass.

THE FAIRVIEW, 1905. The Fairview, constructed in 1842, was the first summer hotel built in Gloucester. Smaller compared to the other grand hotels of the time, the Fairview accommodated 65 guests and was known for having boarded many acclaimed authors and artists. Though many of Gloucester's old resorts and hotels have closed, the Fairview has uniquely remained open since its establishment and currently operates as the Fairview Inn.

THE DELPHINE, EAST GLOUCESTER, MASS.

THE HOTEL DELPHINE, 1920. Built in 1874 in East Gloucester, the Hotel Delphine was one of the earlier hotels built in the area and was in close proximity to Gloucester Harbor. Its original building had 25 rooms, but it expanded, and a new building that could hold 100 guests was built around the early 20th century. Later, it became the Eastern Point Hotel before eventually closing and becoming the site of private apartments.

PAVILION BEACH, 1905. Pavilion Beach was named for the former Pavilion Hotel, Gloucester's first luxury summer resort, which later became known as the Surfside Hotel. Located behind the Pavilion Hotel, Pavilion Beach stretched adjacent to downtown Gloucester to an area called "the fort." Even after the Pavilion Hotel's name was changed and the Surfside Hotel burned down, Pavilion Beach still kept its name and is presently located directly next to Stacy Boulevard.

THE SURFSIDE, 1910. Built in 1849 and known for its upscale charm and beachside access, this building was originally named the Pavilion Hotel and was the first of Gloucester's large luxury resorts. It also later became a recruitment station for Union soldiers during the Civil War and was renamed the Surfside Hotel in 1878. It remained under that name but eventually caught fire on October 17, 1914, and burned down, closing permanently.

THE BEACHCROFT HOUSE (ABOVE) AND HOTEL DOCK, 1920. The Beachcroft House, commonly known as the Beachcroft, was built in 1884 and was initially called the Seaside Hotel. It was formerly located in the Eastern Point area of Gloucester and operated along Niles Beach. The Beachcroft was within easy walking distance to a Gloucester electric streetcar system stop, making it popular for visitors to stay there since they could access other areas of the city with ease. Additionally, its access to a clean and well-maintained beach was well advertised by its proprietors. Other features of the hotel included 90 boarding rooms and a boating dock hotel patrons could access. Like many other Gloucester resorts, the Beachcroft operated seasonally during the summer months but eventually burned down. After its destruction, a private apartment complex was built on the hotel's former site.

The Harbor View, East Gloucester, Mass.

THE HARBOR VIEW, 1905. The Harbor View was built in 1882, and though a seasonal hotel, it was open longer than many of Gloucester's resorts, holding operations from April to November each year. Known especially for its views of Wonson Cove, the hotel grew from being just a boardinghouse to holding eight total buildings at its peak. Popular among artists and even politicians, the hotel remained open until it burned down in 1962.

Hawthorne Inn, East Gloucester, Mass.

THE HAWTHORNE INN, 1905. Built in 1886 and located in the Rocky Neck area of Gloucester, the Hawthorne Inn consisted of 23 buildings, and at its peak, it had approximately 500 boarding rooms. It operated for five decades, but in 1938, several main buildings of the hotel fell victim to arson and were destroyed. Though some buildings survived the blaze, the hotel eventually closed. Presently, the Hawthorne Point Condominiums sit on the hotel's former site.

The Moorland, Bass Rocks, Gloucester, Mass.

THE MOORLAND, 1904 (ABOVE) AND 1905. Built in 1897, the Moorland Hotel was made up of a large complex featuring cottages, an annex, and the actual hotel building. Additionally, the hotel, which operated between the months of June and September, featured a cocktail lounge and grand dining hall, as well as other recreational activities available to guests. Furthermore, the Moorland Hotel was especially popular due to its isolated nature, which oversaw immaculate views of the Atlantic Ocean. The hotel suffered a large fire in 1958, and though some of the complex's buildings survived the blaze, the Moorland Hotel closed down, and many of these buildings were sold or altered. Though under different names, several buildings from the former hotel, such as the old Moorland Annex, still exist today.

The Moorland, Bass Rocks, Gloucester, Mass.

THE ROCKAWAY HOTEL, EAST GLOUCESTER, MASS.   123452

THE ROCKAWAY, 1920. Initially built in the 1850s as the Rackliffe Homestead, this building became the Rockaway Hotel in 1896 when the home was sold and greatly expanded. Located near the Rocky Neck Causeway, the Rockaway held its own pier and was in arm's reach of Gloucester's steamships and electric trolley system. After being exteriorly redesigned several times, the hotel eventually closed by the 1980s, and its building was altered to become condominiums.

Hotel Thorwald, Bass Rocks, Gloucester, Mass.

THE HOTEL THORWALD, 1915. The Thorwald was built along the Bass Rocks section of Gloucester in 1899. Along with many of Gloucester's seaside hotels at the time, it was known for its elegance and luxury, and it featured gardens and covered pathways. After operating for 66 years, it caught fire in 1965 and was severely damaged. It was demolished in 1966, and the Thorwald Condominium was later developed on the site in 1973.

THE COLONIAL ARMS, E. GLOUCESTER. MASS

THE COLONIAL ARMS, 1905 (ABOVE), AND THE LANDING AT COLONIAL ARMS, 1906. Located on Eastern Point, the Colonial Arms was one of the most elegantly designed of Gloucester's seaside resorts, with architectural inspirations from Renaissance influences, but it was also the shortest-lived resort in the Gloucester area. With construction finalized in 1904, the resort featured 300 rooms with telephone connection, including 75 suites, as well as a private boating dock and walkways. A modern and high-class establishment, the Colonial Arms catered to wealthy summer visitors and even hosted events such as banquets and "motor parties." However, the Colonial Arms caught fire on New Year's Eve 1918 and burned down completely.

Gloucester, Mass,   *This taken from Colonial arms*   5660 The Landing Colonial Arms

PUBLISHED BY EDWIN C. MCINTIRE, GLOUCESTER, MASS.

The Ramparts, Eastern Point, Gloucester, Mass.

THE RAMPARTS, 1920. This site initially held the Eastern Point Fort, in use from 1863 to 1867, which protected Gloucester against Confederate attacks from the coast. Later, in the early 1920s, a luxury hotel featuring stone towers called the Ramparts was built in the former earthworks of the fort, which were saved. After three decades of operations, the site was largely razed in 1950, and a private residence was built on the property.

THE TAVERN, GLOUCESTER, MASS.

THE TAVERN, 1935. The Tavern on the Harbor was built in 1920 and featured a well-known restaurant as well as boarding rooms. Located on Western Avenue, "the Tavern," as it is more commonly known, overlooks Gloucester Harbor and the Atlantic Ocean. Still standing today, the property has changed ownership several times and is now operated mostly as an event venue.

THE GARDENS AT GOOD HARBOR BEACH INN, 1935. Situated on the shores of Gloucester, and quite quaint compared to Cape Ann's grand hotels and resorts that were famous in the 1800s and early 1900s, the Good Harbor Beach Inn was established in 1921 and is noted for its unmatched scenery and views of Good Harbor Beach and the Atlantic Ocean, as well as for its beachside gardens and breezeways.

HOTEL SAVOY, GLOUCESTER, MASS.   123879

THE HOTEL SAVOY, 1930. The Hotel Savoy was opened in 1904 by J. Thomas King, a well-known Gloucester hospitality proprietor. Located on the corner of Main and Elm Streets, the hotel was, at one point, Cape Ann's only year-round hotel, and it was known for its fine furnishings and exquisite restaurant. By 1945, its name was changed to the Hotel Gloucester, and it operated under this name until its closure and demolition in 1965.

THE BRYNMERE, 1905. Built in 1885, the Brynmere is located in Annisquam and is known for its views of the Annisquam Harbor. A popular summer resort, it had a thriving business until the 1920s and 1930s, when the area saw a decline in the hospitality industry. Regardless, the Brynmere remained open and underwent considerable downsizing in the 1960s. It is still standing as a hotel in the present day.

THE OVERLOOK, 1905. Built in roughly 1900, the Overlook Hotel, also known as the Grand View Hotel, was another one of Annisquam's bustling lodges. As its name would suggest, the Overlook Hotel was situated on the Annisquam Overlook, a stone barrier that had magnificent views of the Annisquam River. Though knowledge of its history is limited, this hotel is believed to have been closed by the mid-20th century.

CAMP ANNISQUAM, GLOUCESTER, MASS.

CAMP ANNISQUAM, 1940. Camp Annisquam, located directly on the banks of the Annisquam River, was founded in 1923 by Abraham Resnick, a Russian immigrant, who purchased the land where the camp sits to create a family-friendly and affordable vacation spot for tourists visiting Cape Ann. The camp featured several cabins, a large kitchen, and several recreation areas for guests, as well as sponsored dinners and concerts for patrons. Guests could also receive tours of the many hiking and fishing spots the camping site offered. Additionally, Camp Annisquam was uniquely known for being one of the only places on Cape Ann at the time that did not discriminate against Jewish people and as a place where all could congregate without fear of discrimination. Camp Annisquam closed in 1994 and is known in the present day as the Little River Campground.

OCEAN SIDE HOTEL, MAGNOLIA, MASS.

THE OCEANSIDE, 1906. The Oceanside was the second luxury resort that opened in Magnolia and was constructed between 1878 and 1879, opening in the latter year. The Oceanside stood at six stories tall and featured 400 rooms, a recreational area, and a botanical garden. It catered to wealthier clientele from larger cities, such as Boston and New York City, who often vacationed on Cape Ann during warmer months. The resort grew several times and eventually added a tennis court as well as a bar and grill by 1910. At one point, it was the second-largest hotel in New England. It became a landmark due to its size and elegance and because it drew celebrities to the area who patronized the resort, making it the best-known of Magnolia's luxury hotels. Sadly, after eight decades of operation, it caught fire in 1958 and burned down to its foundation, completely destroying it. It was never rebuilt.

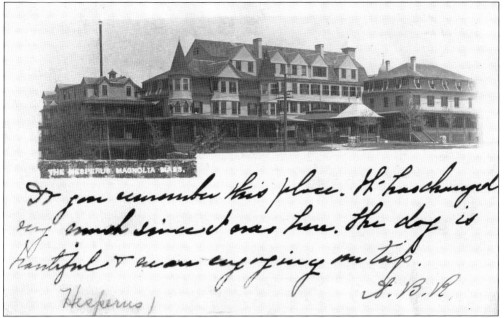

THE HESPERUS, 1906. The Hesperus was Magnolia's first luxury resort and was constructed in 1877. Standing five stories tall, it was briefly the largest hotel in the area before the Oceanside opened, and with its elegant charm, amenities, and scenic views, it aided Magnolia in becoming a popular New England tourist destination. Unfortunately, the Hesperus was demolished in the 1940s after falling into disrepair, and the area where it sat was eventually redeveloped.

THE NEW MAGNOLIA, 1905. Constructed in 1891, the New Magnolia was the last-built and the shortest-lived of Magnolia's luxury hotels. It was located on the southwestern side of Magnolia near Manchester and featured several lounges, a restaurant, and hundreds of boarding rooms. After operating for only 17 total years, it burned down in 1908 and was never rebuilt.

WINGAERSHEEK BEACH, 1920. Though the origins of its name are uncertain and are said to come from broken Dutch or indigenous linguistic influences, Wingaersheek Beach was first surveyed by Europeans in 1627, when Gov. John Endicott (also spelled Endecott) mapped the area as a potential plantation. In the 1600s and 1700s, the area, also known as Coffin's Beach, was used for farming before becoming a Gloucester-run public beach by the 20th century.

GOOD HARBOR BEACH, 1905. Easily one of the most popular beaches in Gloucester among locals and visitors alike, Good Harbor Beach was initially known as Harbor Beach and was once the site of a quaint fishing village. However, toward the late 1800s, when this vicinity began to develop, Good Harbor Beach became a sought-after place to swim, boat, and enjoy summer weather.

LONG BEACH, 1905. Known for stretching between the coasts of Gloucester and Rockport and giving views of the Thacher Island Lighthouses, Long Beach is adorned with numerous cottages and summer homes that have made it a popular choice for tourists and locals to visit. Additionally, while Cape Ann was a tourist hotspot in the early 20th century, the beach was home to the Long Beach Pavilion, an immensely popular local attraction.

THE PAVILION AT LONG BEACH, 1930. Built in 1895 and separate from the former Pavilion Hotel (which became The Surfside), the Long Beach Pavilion was a popular tourist spot in Gloucester, featuring a restaurant, theater, dancing room, and bowling alley. The Pavilion was also a stop on the former Gloucester and Rockport Trolley while it existed. After decades of operation, the Pavilion suffered fire damage on several occasions and was demolished by the 1960s.

East Gloucester, Mass. - Gate Lodge

THE GATE LODGE, 1905. As the Eastern Point section of Gloucester once mainly catered to wealthy socialites, the Eastern Point Associates had the Gate Lodge constructed in 1888 to privatize the area. The Gate Lodge operated on Niles Beach and housed a porter who vetted incoming visitors. Later, as the area developed and was not secluded as a private beach area anymore, the Gate Lodge was sold, and it is now a private residence.

NILES BEACH, EAST GLOUCESTER, MASS.

NILES BEACH, 1920. Niles Beach was initially part of Niles Farm, a 450-acre farm that overlooked Gloucester's seashore and was originally owned by Thomas Niles, a man who also blocked the public from entering Eastern Point after buying most of its land. Purchased by the Eastern Point Associates in 1887, once Gloucester gained a reputation as a summer tourist destination, Niles Beach became the site of several summer resorts and numerous cottages.

CRESSY'S BEACH, 1935. Located on the lower end of Gloucester's famed and historic Stage Fort Park, Cressy's Beach overlooks Gloucester Harbor and is also popular for its picturesque, rocky shoreline. Additionally, the beach was used by early Gloucester settlers to catch, dry, and prepare fish before eventually becoming a recreational site by the 1900s.

HALF MOON BEACH, 1920. Similar to Cressy's Beach, Half Moon Beach is located within Stage Fort Park and is also a much smaller beach compared to the other popular beaches of Gloucester and Cape Ann. Still, this beach is a popular choice for recreationalists, as it is secluded with large rocks bordering its sandy boundaries.

TABLET ADDITION TO STAGE FORT, 1907. After Stage Fort Park opened in 1905, a bronze tablet was added to the Stage Fort Rock that discusses Gloucester's early history. The rock is the park's hallmark but also served as a protective shield for an active fort that existed until 1898. When the tablet was added to the rock on August 16, 1907, the City of Gloucester celebrated with a festival attended by nearly 2,000 Gloucester residents.

STAGE FORT PARK TABLET STATEMENT, 1935. The Stage Fort Park Tablet, added to the Stage Fort Rock (now known as "Tablet Rock") on August 15, 1907, was cast by Eric Pate, a local Essex County resident. The plaque, cast in bronze and measuring a total of 65 square feet, records a historical description of the first permanent settlement in the Massachusetts Bay Colony and commemorates Gloucester's founding in 1623.

STAGE FORT PARK RENOVATION, 1930. In 1930, Stage Fort Park, which had opened 25 years earlier, was renovated for tourism purposes, which saw the park receive time-period cannons and the creation of a cement walking area. In 1973, further renovations occurred, and more original and reproduction cannons were added, as well as a protected walking path along the shore.

STAGE FORT PARK, 1960. After the 1930 renovation of Stage Fort Park, other renovations followed in the decades to come as needed to repair or modernize the park, with the most notable renovation occurring in 1973. This renovation updated the park to its current state and saw the implementation of various walkways and sidewalks, replica cannons, and more metal rails.

MOTHER ANN, 1908. Mother Ann is a rock formation located along Eastern Point in Gloucester that is noted for its scenic beauty and unique view that gives the impression of a reclining woman. Said to have been named by sailor William Thompson in 1891, the formation is often thought to represent a female Puritan settler or Anne of Denmark, the former queen of England and Ireland, for whom Cape Ann is also named.

BRACE'S ROCK AND OLD SALT, 1907. Located outside of Gloucester Harbor, Brace's Rock (also called Bracy's Rock or Brase's Rock) is a large rock located several hundred feet in the Atlantic Ocean that has been the site of numerous shipwrecks during Cape Ann's maritime history. This has served as the inspiration behind the inclusion in this image of "Old Salt," who represents all of Gloucester's hardworking fishermen who regularly faced dangerous voyages at sea.

Five

THE TIP OF THE CAPE
VIEWS OF ROCKPORT

Originally settled by Richard Tarr as the Sandy Bay Colony in approximately 1690, Rockport was initially a fishing community that capitalized off the town's natural harbor. Additionally, as the colony continued to grow in the ensuing decades, it thrived off the pine timber and turpentine industries as those two products were needed to build ships and schooners, another instrument in making the region's fishing and maritime industry as successful as it was. Furthermore, in the 1700s, more settlers established homesteads in Sandy Bay, continuing the colony's growth and designation as its own enclave on Cape Ann. However, the Sandy Bay Colony was made a parish of Gloucester in 1756 and annexed into that town's borders. Though Sandy Bay became a section of Gloucester instead of its own community at that point, similar growth continued throughout the next century, and the colony's maritime lifestyle and economy especially flourished with the establishment of the Rockport Harbor and Breakwater, the creation of the Thacher Island Lighthouses, and the further success of the Sandy Bay fisheries.

In the mid-1800s, well-established as its own thriving community, the people of Sandy Bay voted to secede from Gloucester and establish the town of Rockport, which was incorporated on February 27, 1840. This marked a transformation for the town because it was no longer a part of Gloucester, but also because this period saw the establishment of the region's granite industry, which would provide immense financial support to citizens in this community for the next century to come, especially for the many of whom worked in the town's quarries and granite processing factories, such as the Rockport Granite Company. Eventually, this industry too became less popular in Rockport and dwindled, but Rockport soon became another beacon of Cape Ann's hospitality industry with the formation of several resorts in the town that drew those involved with the fine arts. This has continued an everlasting legacy in Rockport, as in the years since, Rockport has become an artist's haven and an eclectic community that boasts numerous galleries, restaurants, stores, historical sites, and hospitality enterprises in the present day, especially along Bearskin Neck and its downtown area.

VIEW OF ROCKPORT HARBOR, 1905. When Rockport was initially founded as the Sandy Bay Colony, colonists immediately turned to maritime means to help establish a steady economy for the community. Once constructed, a successful fishing operation began at Rockport Harbor, making it a vital source of revenue for the town. Additionally, the harbor is historically significant to Rockport as it holds many of the town's historic buildings and has been featured in numerous artworks.

ROCKPORT HARBOR BREAKWATER, 1960. In 1882, the US Congress granted a survey of the former Sandy Bay Harbor (now Rockport Harbor) for the construction of a breakwater. Construction began in 1886, but by 1898, though much money and granite had been invested in the project, storms destroyed the partially complete breakwater. After obstacles hindered the breakwater's construction in the ensuing years, the project was eventually deemed infeasible, and the breakwater's construction was abandoned in 1916.

THE YACHT CLUB AND HARBOR FROM ATLANTIC AVENUE, ROCKPORT, MASS.—R40

ROCKPORT YACHT CLUB, 1945. The Sandy Bay Yacht Club, now the Rockport Yacht Club, was established in 1885, soon after a greater interest in yachting and recreational sailing grew across the nation. Located along Rockport Harbor, it initially started as a sailing organization. The club has held regattas and sponsored numerous community events in Rockport since its inception over a century ago.

END OF THE DAY AT MOTIF NO. 1, ROCKPORT, MASS.—R45

MOTIF NO. ONE, 1945. Motif No. 1, located on Bearskin Neck, is one of Rockport's most iconic landmarks. The building, a red fisherman's shack, was built in 1840. Since Rockport has consistently been an artist's haven, the building was the muse of numerous maritime-themed artworks about the area, which gained it notoriety. It was destroyed in the Blizzard of 1978, and an exact replica of the building was constructed that same year.

BEARSKIN NECK, 1945 (ABOVE) AND 1965. Bearskin Neck, a small strip of land that jets out into Rockport Harbor, was once home to bears that were hunted by settlers in the town's early years, which is the official inspiration for Bearskin Neck's name. As Bearskin Neck was settled once the wildlife threats ceased, it became a bustling center for Rockport's granite and fishing industries in the 1800s as well. However, in the past century, upon the downfall of both industries on Cape Ann, Bearskin Neck has become a top attraction in the town due to its proximity to Rockport's sights and downtown area. Additionally, it has grown a reputation for being an artist's haven and has become a center for fine arts, shopping, and restaurants, largely contributing to Rockport's tourism economy.

DOCK SQUARE, ROCKPORT, 1950. Located in downtown Rockport at the intersection of Main and Mount Pleasant Streets, Dock Square aids in Rockport's general reputation of being the site of an eclectic fine arts and culture scene, hosting numerous charming, Colonial-era buildings significant to Rockport's general history as well as many art galleries, quaint shops, and restaurants.

CLEAVES STREET, ROCKPORT, 1920. Originally planned in 1855, Cleaves Street was named for members of the influential Cleaves family of Rockport. Located off Jewett Street in northwestern Rockport, Cleaves Street is the site of numerous cottages and Rockport's congregation of the Unitarian Universalist church. It borders "Old Sloop," another one of Rockport's historic churches, as well.

The Post Office, Rockport, Mass.

ROCKPORT POST OFFICE, 1940. During the Great Depression, the New Deal program was implemented to help fund infrastructure and public projects and to relieve economic distress and unemployment. The town of Rockport benefited from this program, as it funded the Rockport Post Office's construction, along with several other buildings. Built in 1938, the post office is still in operation and features a mural painted in 1939 that is dedicated to the New Deal program.

CARNEGIE LIBRARY, ROCKPORT. MASS.

CARNEGIE LIBRARY, ROCKPORT, 1910. Rockport's first library was established in 1871 in a small space at the Rockport Town Hall. After the library outgrew this space, Andrew Carnegie, a wealthy industrialist, gave funds to Rockport to build a new library. Following negotiations, plans to build a Carnegie library in Rockport were approved in 1903. Now a private residence, the library opened in 1907 and operated until 1993, when it moved into the former Tarr Schoolhouse.

ANNISQUAM COTTON MILL RUINS, 1903. The Annisquam Cotton Mill began operations in 1847 in Rockport and added several buildings to its complex throughout its time of operation. The mill was one of the largest cotton mills in Massachusetts, and in total, the mill operated for 35 years before it burned down in 1882. The ruins of the mill stood for over 20 years before most buildings were demolished in 1904.

GEORGE J. TARR SCHOOL BUILDING, 1907. This building, constructed in 1864, was initially part of the Annisquam Cotton Mill. Though most of the mill burned down in 1882, this particular building survived the blaze. The mill's ruins were demolished in 1904, but the owner of the property, George Tarr, deeded this surviving building to the Town of Rockport, which made it a school in his honor. The building became the town library in 1993.

THE FIRST CHURCH, SOMETIMES CALLED "THE OLD SLOOP"
ROCKPORT, MASS.

OLD SLOOP CHURCH, ROCKPORT, 1920. The First Congregational Church of Rockport, also called "Old Sloop" (a nickname given to it by local fishermen), established its congregation in 1755. As wars prevented the townsfolk from having a permanent church building, this structure was built in 1805, fifty years after its congregation was formed. In the years since, this church has served as a gathering place for Rockport residents, and it is a vital part of the community's history.

THE STEEPLE AT OLD SLOOP CHURCH, 1955. During the War of 1812, the bell in Old Sloop's steeple was rung to alarm Sandy Bay residents of British attacks. During one attack, British forces fired on the bell to stop its sound, but they hit the steeple instead. Though the steeple was kept in place and was eventually repaired and enlarged to its current state, in 1840, the steeple's bell was moved to the former Riverdale Methodist Meetinghouse in Gloucester.

THE JAMES BABSON SHOP, 1925. The James Babson Shop is Rockport's oldest structure and is estimated to have been built in 1658. The land the building sits on was bought by the Babson family in the first recorded land grant in Rockport, and it was initially used as a cooperage. It changed ownership several times over the succeeding centuries before it became a museum in 1931, which is how it stands today.

THE ROCKPORT NEWSPAPER HOUSE, 1920. Built between 1922 and 1924 by Elis F. Stenman, a native of Sweden, the "Paper House" is a wooden-frame home built using hundreds of sheets of varnished newspaper as its insulation. Additionally, varnished newspaper was used for decorating the home's walls and to construct the majority of the home's furniture. After the home's construction, it quickly became a tourist attraction, and it is now maintained as a museum.

Rockport Granite Co's. Wharf,
Rockport, Mass.

ROCKPORT GRANITE QUARRIES, 1912 (ABOVE), AND BRIDGE AT ROCKPORT GRANITE QUARRIES, 1915. By the 1830s, Rockport began to be known for more than its fishing economy, as it was quickly becoming one of the biggest granite-producing areas in the nation. The granite industry, which led to the creation of numerous quarries in the Rockport vicinity, contributed to local wealth, as it helped create many jobs, especially with the numerous companies that established operations in the area. Cape Ann granite was mainly used for construction and paving projects across the nation as well as around the world, which helped the region gain further wealth and notoriety before the granite industry declined by the early 20th century.

Stone Bridge at Granite Quarries, Rockport, Mass.

VIEW OF PIGEON COVE, 1905. A little over one mile northwest of Rockport, Pigeon Cove is a small community settled in approximately 1702 that was an important granite-producing center in the early years of its existence. Though known for its contributions to Cape Ann's industrial success, by the 1800s, Pigeon Cove gained a reputation as a summer resort area and was also known for its maritime industry.

THE WITCH HOUSE, 1910. One of Rockport's oldest homes, the "Witch House," also known as the "Garrison House," is believed to have been constructed as a defense post during King Philip's War in 1676. However, stories say a Salem family built it in 1692 to hide a relative accused of witchcraft. Regardless, it became a boardinghouse in the 1800s and eventually was bought for use as a private residence, which it remains today.

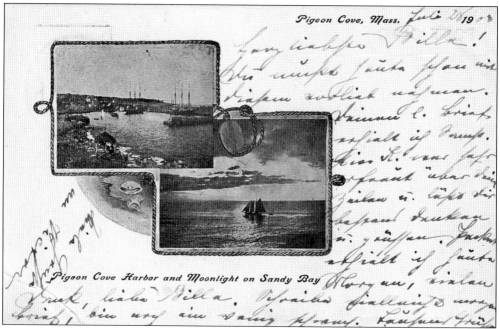

Pigeon Cove, Mass.

Pigeon Cove Harbor and Moonlight on Sandy Bay

PIGEON COVE AND ITS HARBOR, 1903. As Pigeon Cove continued to grow in the 1800s and become a sought-after area for summer retreatists, the community developed a residential area, churches, businesses, and an active harbor that offered maritime recreational activities, such as boating and yachting, and maintained a busy fishing port that rivaled other local harbors.

Photo. Only, Copyright 1905 by the Rotograph Co.

G 7176   Halibut Point, Pigeon Cove, Mass.

Rockport, Mass., July 29, 1908.

Dear Mildred, – We are at Rockport and having a great time, bathing, sailing and driving. Wish you would write to me.
Theresa I Cram

HALIBUT POINT, 1905. Halibut Point once held the Babson Farm quarry, which was home to granite over 400 million years old. Eventually bought by the Rockport Granite Company, the quarry ceased operations in 1929. It later became the Halibut Point Reservation in 1934 when more land was purchased to expand the property. In 1981, the State of Massachusetts purchased the reservation and established it as the Halibut Point State Park.

Six

Cape Ann's
Quaint Village
Views of Essex

Essex, though the smallest town on Cape Ann, has a rich history dating back to its establishment in 1634, eleven years after Cape Ann's first European settlement was founded at present-day Gloucester. Originally part of Ipswich, Essex was first known as "southern Ipswich" or "Chebacco," the latter name being derived from Lake Chebacco, which borders Essex, as well as for the Native American tribe that resided in the area. After being part of Ipswich for nearly 200 years, even though the community later maintained a separate meetinghouse and church, Essex was officially incorporated as its own town in 1819. Similar to other communities on Cape Ann, Essex's early economy, during the Colonial era, thrived on the maritime industry, mostly through shipbuilding and fishing. Furthermore, Essex played a significant role in the shipbuilding industry, and over 4,000 vessels were produced in the town, such as fishing schooners and recreational watercraft. The fishing schooners produced in Essex were especially important to Gloucester's economy; many Gloucester fishermen used these vessels for their voyages, resulting in these two communities relying on each other to ensure the region's success in the maritime industry. Though the shipbuilding industry in Essex is not as necessary to the town's survival as it once was, many enterprises in Essex still continue the town's legacy in the shipbuilding sector. Furthermore, the Essex Shipbuilding Museum, founded in 1976, preserves the town's shipbuilding history and heritage and represents the skills of many craftsmen throughout Essex's history.

Even though the maritime industry is not as prevalent as it once was on the general Cape Ann peninsula, Essex still maintains its quaint charm but, in more recent decades, has grown its downtown area to include numerous restaurants on the shore of the Essex River, many of which specialize in shellfish preparation, for which the town is known. Additionally, in more recent decades, Essex has grown to be a hotspot for antiques enthusiasts, proudly boasting the distinction of being one of the best antiquing destinations in the United States due to the presence of numerous well-established antiques stores within its town limits.

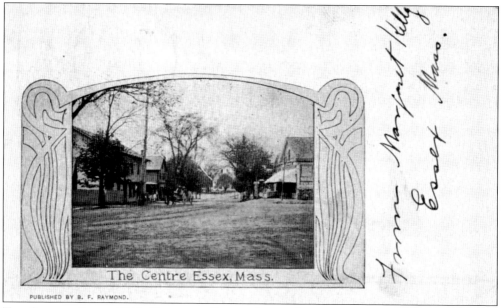

The Centre Essex, Mass.

PUBLISHED BY B. F. RAYMOND.

THE CENTRE, ESSEX, 1904. Downtown Essex is known for its quaint nature, serving as the site of many churches and rustic Colonial homes, as well as being the setting for town functions. Additionally, this area is home to numerous antiques stores that have given the town the designation of being a destination for antiques dealers and collectors alike.

Village Center Showing U.S. Postoffice. Essex, Mass.

VILLAGE CENTER, ESSEX, 1965. In addition to holding a quiet yet well-established downtown, Essex is also home to two different villages that make up a census-designated place on the outskirts of its borders, which is also named Essex. However, the Village Center, which was located in Essex's southern village, was home to many restaurants, storefronts, attractions, and a post office.

110

MAIN STREET, ESSEX, 1905. Though Main Street in Essex was a once rural road that stretched over the marshy estuaries that border the town, it has grown over the past century, becoming the home of numerous acclaimed seafood restaurants along the banks of the Essex River (especially ones that specialize in preparing clams and shellfish), as well as antiques stores, churches, and older homes that line the roadway.

ESSEX HIGH SCHOOL, 1905. Essex does not hold many public schools of its own, as it is a small town with a lighter population, especially compared to the municipalities that surround it. Essex's first high school was constructed in the late 1800s in a two-story building styled similarly to a home. Though its history is limited, it is believed to no longer be in existence.

4738   Town Hall & Soldiers' Monument,
Essex, Mass.

SOLDIERS' MONUMENT, ESSEX, MASS.
Published by B. F. Raymond

ESSEX TOWN HALL AND SOLDIERS' MONUMENT, 1906. The Essex Town Hall was designed by architect Frank Weston and constructed between 1893 and 1894 with funds donated by Thomas Oliver Hazard Perry "T.O.H.P." Burnham, an Essex native and wealthy Boston businessman. The town hall contains the town's municipal offices, an auditorium, and the T.O.H.P. Burnham Public Library. All of these offices and resources continue to presently operate in the building, which underwent a massive renovation in 2017.

ESSEX SOLDIERS' MONUMENT, 1905. Next to the Essex Town Hall in Memorial Park stands the Essex Soldiers' Monument, which was made in 1905 from granite derived from Ames and Snow, a local company that operated in Rockport. Though seen as a memorial to all soldiers, the monument's specific purpose was to honor soldiers from the US Civil War.

CONGREGATIONAL CHURCH, ESSEX, MASS.

Essex Congregational Church, 1905. Long before Essex was known by its current name, the town was referred to as "Chebacco," named for the lake in the vicinity and because that is what the southern area of Ipswich was called at the time. In 1679, residents of the Chebacco community were granted permission to construct their own church building and meetinghouse. Made of logs, it was finished in 1683. This log church building did not last long before the second church building was constructed in the early 1700s, followed by the third building in 1753. The last and current church, which is still used by the congregation today, was built in 1792.

ESSEX METHODIST CHURCH, 1940. Thought to have been initially constructed in 1809 as a building used by the Christian Society, an at-the-time socially progressive religious organization, the former Methodist Episcopal church on Eastern Avenue in Essex was in operation here from the time of its construction to approximately the early 2000s. Decommissioned as a church for several decades now, the building was purchased and is now privately owned.

CHURCH OF ST. JOHN THE BAPTIST, 1940. Formerly, Catholics in Essex had to travel to Gloucester to worship, but in 1918, the Archdiocese of Boston created a mission of the St. Ann Parish in Essex, which became St. John the Baptist Catholic Church in 1931. In 1951, the first church building, seen above, was demolished and replaced by a new building, hall, and sanctuary on the same site. The church's original rectory was demolished in 2021.

CHOATE HOUSE, (BUILT IN 1725) CHOATE ISLAND,
ESSEX RIVER, ESSEX, MASS.

CHOATE HOUSE, 1914. Built in approximately 1730, the Choate House was originally owned by Rufus Choate, an Essex County native and US senator from Massachusetts. Located on the isolated and remote Choate Island, the house is only accessible by boat. It is now part of the Crane National Wildlife Refuge and is presently owned by the Trustees of Reservations organization.

LAUNCHING A FISHING SCHOONER, ESSEX, 1920. The town of Essex is known for its immense contributions to the shipbuilding industry, as over 4,000 vessels have been built in the town in the past four centuries of its existence. In the 1800s, the town began to be known for its successful production of fishing schooners. After these schooners were "landed" at Essex, many were sent to Gloucester to be used in fishing voyages by local fishermen.

Robin's View on Essex River, Essex, Mass. Island.

VIEWS OF CONOMO POINT, 1914. Located along the marshy estuaries of Essex Bay, Conomo Point was first the site of a poor farm, an early term for a public-run home for poorer individuals. By the late 1800s, Conomo Point became an active recreational waterfront center that many hunters and fishermen came to utilize before the neighborhood became a summer tourist destination by 1900 with the construction of numerous cottages and summer residences.

Road View at Conomo, Chebacco River, Essex, Mass. around the point

VIEW OF LAKE CHEBACCO, 1940. Named for the Native American tribe that inhabited the vicinity, Lake Chebacco (also known as Chebacco Lake) is a lake located in Essex that is known for its immense support to the town's early fishing industry. Additionally, the lake was used for freshwater ice harvesting, and it was also a source of revenue for town residents before becoming a recreational spot amidst the growth of the region in the 20th century.

General View of Lake Chebacco, Essex, Mass.

Seven

Coves and Cottages
Views of Manchester-by-the-Sea

Sitting on land that previously belonged to the Algonquin Native Americans, Manchester-by-the-Sea is a small community founded in 1629 in a land grant from England's King Charles I. The town, initially known as Jeoffereye's Creek when English settlers first arrived, was founded from parts of Salem and Gloucester. It was technically a part of Salem during its early existence, and after spending 16 years as a settlement, it was incorporated as its own village in 1645, gaining its first official name of Manchester at that time (the town's name was officially changed to Manchester-by-the-Sea, an old nickname for Manchester, in 1989). Like most municipalities and villages in the Cape Ann region, Manchester-by-the-Sea's harbor was popular due to its short distance from Salem, Boston, and Gloucester. It was a frequent stop for many ships and became a rival to nearby harbors as well, cementing its status as its own successful fishing community.

However, Manchester-by-the-Sea shifted from the fishing sector toward the blooming hospitality industry in the 1800s and eventually became another one of the region's summer hotspots for wealthy tourists by the beginning of the 20th century. Though most of the luxury summer resorts were located in Gloucester and in other areas of northern Cape Ann, tourists still chose Manchester-by-the-Sea as the site to construct summer cottages and residences, for which the town became known. Furthermore, Manchester-by-the-Sea's close proximity to Magnolia, a community in southern Gloucester noted for its elegant nature, led to the development of other high-end and upscale businesses and enterprises within the town's borders.

Nevertheless, Manchester-by-the-Sea's tourist economy eventually declined in the mid-20th century, at the time when the popularity of most of Cape Ann's hospitality sector also began to recede. However, the town still retained many upscale elements that led a wealthy summer population to maintain their residences there. The town's other sites, such as Masconomo Park, Singing Beach, Eagle Head, Pickwith Point, and the Coolidge Reservation, also continue to draw tourists, along with those who enjoy Manchester-by-the-Sea's historic charm due to the numerous Colonial-style buildings, old cottages, storefronts, and churches that line the town's streets.

AERIAL VIEW OF MANCHESTER HARBOR, 1935. Manchester-by-the-Sea is naturally located on a cove (known as Proctor Cove) and an inlet. In the town's early days, the Manchester Harbor was a rival to nearby seaside towns such as Gloucester and Salem, and it was a vital local fishing port from the 1600s to the 1800s. In the present day, the harbor remains busy and is home to numerous fishing docks and private mooring areas.

SINGING BEACH, 1906. Situated between Eagle Head and Pickwith Point, two local rock formations, Singing Beach is known for its clean waters and "singing sands," which make noise in the wind and which gave the beach its name. Located toward Magnolia and Gloucester, Singing Beach also allows public access and boasts views of Salt Island from its shores as well.

VIEWS OF MANCHESTER-BY-THE-SEA, 1903. By the late 1800s and early 1900s, Manchester-by-the-Sea was the site of many municipal buildings, churches, and elegant cottages that garnered the attention of tourists and locals in the area. Many of these sites, such as the former town hall, were known for their unique architectural elements, which had only increased the town's popularity.

TOWN HALL, MANCHESTER-BY-THE-SEA, 1908. Manchester-by-the-Sea's first town hall was built in 1868 and served as the town's center for municipal offices for over a century before being demolished in 1969. The new town hall, located in approximately the same location as the former building, was constructed in 1970 and remains Manchester-by-the-Sea's current town hall today.

Copyright 1905 by the Rotograph Co

G 7164 School St., Manchester-by-the-Sea, Mass

SCHOOL STREET, MANCHESTER-BY-THE-SEA, 1905. School Street in Manchester-by-the-Sea is almost a mile in length and is home to many of the town's historic sites. As School Street begins in downtown Manchester-by-the-Sea, one can notice the older Colonial-style buildings that line the streetscape, as well as numerous elegant homes, businesses, and historic churches along its route.

Post Office, Manchester-by-the-Sea, Mass.

POST OFFICE, MANCHESTER-BY-THE-SEA, 1905. Manchester-by-the-Sea's first post office was built in 1803. This post office was a stone building that took up a whole corner of downtown Manchester, making that area known as "the post office block." This post office also preceded the current post office in Manchester-by-the-Sea, which was constructed in 1940 with funds from the New Deal program and is located on Beach Street.

MASCONOMO PARK, MANCHESTER-BY-THE-SEA, 1905. Named for Masconomo, also known as Masconomet, an Agawam chief who deeded most of the land in Essex County (including Manchester-by-the-Sea) to English settlers in the 1600s, Masconomo Park came into existence in the 1800s and is located off the present-day Beach Street. The park overlooks the Manchester-by-the-Sea Harbor and is the site of many town functions and celebrations.

MANCHESTER-BY-THE-SEA RAIL DEPOT, 1914. The first railroad passenger station in Manchester-by-the-Sea was constructed in August 1847. Like other nearby rails, the Manchester line was owned by the Eastern Railroad before the Boston & Maine Railroad absorbed it. Later, the 1847 depot seen here was replaced in 1895 by a new building that stood until 1977. Additionally, this station operated simultaneously with another depot in the town named West Manchester, which closed by 1940.

PRIEST SCHOOL, C. 1905. The George A. Priest School, built in 1890, was the first multiroom school built in Manchester. Previously, Manchester was served by small, one-room schoolhouses that became quickly outgrown by the mid-1800s. This school building was converted by the 1920s to the Manchester Middle School before it closed in 1967. The building was demolished in 1970.

JOHN PRICE SCHOOL, 1905. The John Price School, commonly known as the "Price School," was an elementary school located on Norwood Avenue and Brook Street in Manchester-by-the-Sea. It remained an elementary school for over 50 years until Manchester's Story High School moved into the building in 1953. The Memorial Elementary School then became the new elementary school at roughly that time. Eventually, the Price School building closed, and it was demolished in 1965.

THE HIGH SCHOOL, MANCHESTER-BY-THE-SEA, 1904. After Manchester-by-the-Sea's public schools were consolidated in the mid-1800s, in 1874, a new high school was established in a pre-existing building located on Bennett Street, seen here. After it was expanded several times, this high school was renamed Story High School in 1895. Story High School was moved to the former Price School building in 1953, and this building was demolished that year.

THE HIGH SCHOOL, MANCHESTER, MASS.

THE G. W. ARMSTRONG D. R. & N. CO., BOSTON

PUBLIC LIBRARY, MANCHESTER-BY-THE-SEA, MASS.

HANDCOLORED

THE PUBLIC LIBRARY, 1906. Manchester's Lyceum Association was created in 1830 after "social libraries" formed by town residents failed. The association soon established the town's Lyceum Library, and after it disbanded in 1871, the town acquired its collections. The Manchester Free Library was soon established on School Street, and after this space was outgrown, a new library building that still exists today was constructed in 1887 with donated funds from Manchester resident Thomas Coolidge.

Congregational Church 1809 and Town Hall
Manchester-by-the-Sea, Mass.

Manchester by the Sea, Mass. Orthodox Church

CONGREGATIONAL CHURCH (ABOVE) AND ORTHODOX CONGREGATIONAL CHURCH, BOTH 1905. Manchester-by-the-Sea's First Congregational Church was established on November 7, 1716, and was the first church in Manchester (as the town was then known). Residents had to travel to Salem and Beverly to attend worship services before this church was built. The church has held services in four total buildings during its existence, but the final and current church building was constructed in 1809 in Manchester's downtown. The church's name was changed to Orthodox Congregational Church in 1843, and in 1844, the church clergy gained full control of the church after splitting ownership with the town, shortly before the church briefly split into two congregations due to disputes in 1857. By 1869, the church congregation was reunited. It changed its name to the First Parish Church Congregational in 1979, by which name it is known today.

Sacred Heart Church and Rectory   Manchester-by-the-Sea, Mass.

SACRED HEART CATHOLIC CHURCH, 1910. Sources state Manchester-by-the-Sea's first Catholic church was constructed off of School Street in 1873. However, the Sacred Heart Catholic Church was built by Irish immigrants on Cape Ann beginning in 1901, and the church, made of stone, was completed in 1905. The church maintained its own congregation until it and the Church of St. John the Baptist in Essex were merged into one church parish in recent years.

Manchester by the Sea, Mass.   Baptist Church

BAPTIST CHURCH, 1905. Located in the downtown area of Manchester-by-the-Sea off of School Street, the former Manchester Baptist Church, built in 1844, is one of the town's oldest churches. Though changed from its original state, the church has been enlarged and has undergone several renovations that altered its appearance. It was eventually renamed the Cornerstone Church.

A 7167 Manchester Yacht Club, Manchester-by-the-Sea, Mass.

MANCHESTER-BY-THE-SEA YACHT CLUB, 1906. Located along Manchester Harbor, the Manchester Yacht Club was founded in 1892 and still maintains its original building there. Along with hosting many boat races and competitive matches, the club also organizes cruises to and from New England and Canada. In addition, the yacht club also maintains a private marina and holds a total membership fleet of over 300 boats.

ESSEX COUNTY CLUB, MANCHESTER.

SERIES A, NO. 7.
L. W. FLOYD, MANCHESTER-BY-THE-SEA.

ESSEX COUNTY COUNTRY CLUB, 1905. Established in downtown Manchester's outskirts on a 180-acre tract of land, the Essex County Country Club and its original clubhouse were created in 1893. Initially only a nine-hole course that also offered numerous sporting amenities, the grounds expanded to a full 18-hole golf course in 1917, and a new clubhouse has since been constructed. It is maintained as a private club and is still in operation today.

BIBLIOGRAPHY

Babson, John. *History of the Town of Gloucester, Cape Ann, Including the Town of Rockport*. Gloucester, MA: Procter Brothers, 1860.

Cape Ann Museum. "Historic Properties." May 19, 2023. https://www.capeannmuseum.org/historic-properties/

Cape Ann Museum. "History of Cape Ann." https://www.capeannmuseum.org/about/history-of-the-museum/history-of-cape-ann/

Essex Coastal Scenic Byway. "Manchester-by-the-Sea, MA." June 3, 2022. https://coastalbyway.org/communities/manchester-by-the-sea/

The Grand Hotels of Gloucester and Cape Ann (blog). Historic Ipswich on the Massachusetts North Shore, April 29, 2023. https://historicipswich.net/2021/09/04/the-grand-hotels-of-gloucester-and-cape-ann-1905/

Greater Cape Ann Chamber of Commerce. https://capeannchamber.com

Gloucester Daily Times, 1888–1981. Sawyer Free Library, https://sawyer.advantage-preservation.com/

Gloucester's Rich History (blog). Discover Gloucester, June 19, 2018. https://discovergloucester.com/2018/06/19/gloucesters-history/

Morreale, Susan, and Richard Carlson. "The Changing Landscape: Summer Hotels of East Gloucester." Historicgloucester.com: A Private Website with History of Gloucester. http://historicgloucester.com/viewer.asp?base_dir=hotels&title=Summer%20Hotels%20of%20East%20Gloucester

Sawyer Free Library. sawyerfreelibrary.org

Suo, Joseph, and Colleen Suo. Train Postcard Collection. Audio-Visual Designs.

Town of Essex, MA. "History of Essex." https://www.essexma.org/about-essex/pages/history

DISCOVER THOUSANDS OF LOCAL HISTORY BOOKS FEATURING MILLIONS OF VINTAGE IMAGES

Arcadia Publishing, the leading local history publisher in the United States, is committed to making history accessible and meaningful through publishing books that celebrate and preserve the heritage of America's people and places.

Find more books like this at
www.arcadiapublishing.com

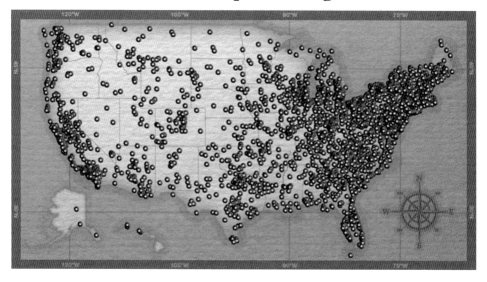

Search for your hometown history, your old stomping grounds, and even your favorite sports team.

Consistent with our mission to preserve history on a local level, this book was printed in South Carolina on American-made paper and manufactured entirely in the United States. Products carrying the accredited Forest Stewardship Council (FSC) label are printed on 100 percent FSC-certified paper.

MADE IN THE USA